Linda D. Jernigan
P.O. Box 612
Richton Park, IL 60471
Email: LJernigan@LindaJernigan.com
Website: LindaJernigan.com

Printed by Kairos Christian Publishing Co.

THE EVANGELISTS ARE COMING
Volume II

Written by: Linda D. Jernigan, M.A.

TABLE OF CONTENT

* PART ONE: EVANGELIST: The Person *

My Evangelistic Discovery
Word to Evangelist: Our Time is Now!
Introduction

* PART TWO: EVANGELISM: The Event *

PART ONE

EVANGELIST: THE PERSON

MY EVANGELISTIC DISCOVERY

*E*vangelist. What does that mean?

That was my agonizing question from the onset of hearing that I was an evangelist.

My preaching ministry began in August 2003 and instantly I was labeled an evangelist. In retrospect, I may have been labeled an evangelist by default because in my denomination all female preachers were called evangelists. If you were a woman who preached, you were an evangelist...no further questions asked! Nevertheless, in my preaching debut as an evangelist, there were about one hundred and fifty people present, primarily family and friends. There was not much jubilation nor celebration but rather mountains of speculation about my evangelistic ministry because I was an ex-lesbian. To say that people were cynical would be a gross understatement; they were most incredulous and unconvinced about my conversion.

However, despite the doubts and disbeliefs of people, I flourished as an itinerant evangelist primarily because I openly shared my personal testimony of deliverance from lesbianism. God anointed me to preach Jesus and graced me to live under the constant suspicious surveillant eye of spectators. As a result, my influence grew wider as the voice of doubters were rampant; most were viciously vocal about their uncertainties concerning my deliverance as if I should not be permitted to operate in ministry because I was a former homosexual. Honestly, I did not challenge their doubts because I had my own doubts intermingled with fear; not about my past or my conversion, but rather about the title of evangelist...what is that?

In 2006, I was officially endorsed as an evangelist by my local church. Being transparent, I did not know what "evangelist" meant nor how I should walk it out. I assumed I would preach about salvation and organize community events. Because I was gifted at both, I embraced the title and office of an evangelist based on the miniscule information I possessed.

Nevertheless, I preached the Gospel with everything in me, and people responded to the invitation to receive Jesus as their Savior. In addition, I organized community outreach events where thousands attended and received natural resources and humanitarian services. God was glorified and I was *somewhat* satisfied. However, I still sought to understand and get revelation about the evangelist; that internal uncertainty arrested my confidence and caused great ministry insecurity, even though vocally I preached and shared my testimony boldly...internally I was insecure!

In 2012, I lived through one of the most significant years of my entire life. I celebrated my birthday in January and earned my Master of Arts degree in May. The church where I served thrived, and my world was near flawless. As the year ended, I had an episode with people dear to my heart. They disagreed with elements of my personal journey, and it became ugly...to the extent where I was physically assaulted. However, as pained as I was about the entire ordeal, I refused to act in a way that would grieve God.

As a fighter who regularly initiated fights and finished fights by any means necessary, on that day I was fully assured I loved God more than anything; even more than being right in the eyes of people and even more than the need to defend myself. In the unpleasantness of that ordeal, God stamped me publicly and openly as an evangelist; an itinerant preaching, revivalist, 21st century evangelist with an apostolic bend! It wasn't done with a parade nor a celebration, but rather my heavenly validation as an evangelist was birthed in extreme pain which required me to travail in anguish for several months.

Soon after that incident, I lost passion for everything...including life. I was severely saddened and deeply discouraged. I contemplated my resignation as a pastor from the church I served because I *labored* to attend church services and perform pastoral duties. I didn't feel like a pastor nor a teacher, not even a Christian.

Soon, the small whispers in my soul slid into screeching screams which forced me to resign. I was tormented! I pondered, "If I was not a pastor, then "WHAT" was I? Frankly, I was afraid to explore the possibility of resigning because my identity had become knotted into my title of a pastor. However, I could not ignore the squeals from my heart. I hesitated to resign as pastor because I dreaded causing disappointment to people who supported me i.e. members of our church, my own pastor, and all the ministers and leaders who believed in me. I did not want to let them down.

Each time I internally asked myself the question, "If I'm not a pastor, then what am I?" I heard, "You are an evangelist." But again, "What is an evangelist?" By that time, I had been actively engaged in ministry and been productive for nearly ten years, but I still did not have clarity on my original title and expected function as evangelist.

I was embarrassed to admit that I was comfortable being a pastor because that was an acceptable and respected title in Christian churches. Everyone knew what a pastor was, unlike an evangelist. The fog of an evangelist frightened me. To be honest, it was a world I did not want to explore because being an evangelist lacked prestige, without any celebrations, no applauses, and was void of the spotlight. It was like being in custodial work where you are invisible until needed i.e. something gets clogged and/or not working properly.

My observation was that most evangelists did not have a visible role inside church but were expected to be outside of church doing intense grinding for the sole benefit of the church, which was to increase attendance. It felt like churches did not honor the Biblical, Ephesians 4:12 contribution of the evangelist inside of the church, which was to perfect (mature) and edify (teach/build up) church members. Naw babe, that's not for me…I'll just stay in my comfortable pastor's role, attend church, and stay safe in my religious Christian bubble of acceptance.

After months of internal deliberation and negotiation, I realized I feared being an evangelist because I had little knowledge of an evangelist. Unbelievable! I had little knowledge of the title which I proudly posted on my business cards, website, and the title which I demanded people call me. Therefore, when God allowed the unique circumstances of 2012 to occur, I felt confronted by God and I was like a mouse caught in a mouse trap jammed, squealing, and fighting for my life.

As a result, I ran to my lifeline, the Bible! I decided to conduct an exhaustive Biblical study of the evangelist. Frankly, in my heart I studied the evangelist to silence the internal voices but mainly to *prove* to myself that I was indeed a pastor.

Unannounced to me, the King James Version (KJV) Bible only had three Scriptural references where the actual word "Evangelist" appeared…three *measly* Scriptures! Acts 21:8, Ephesians 4:11, and 2 Timothy 4:5, none of which discussed the attributes or characteristics of an evangelist nor the role of an evangelist in the Christian church. I was incredibly dissatisfied.

How could I evaluate myself to determine if I was an evangelist or not? I earnestly desired to answer that question once and for all…was I an evangelist or a pastor? I was more confused and discombobulated because as I looked further into my bag of gifts, I also saw strong prophetic winds blowing and in operation within me as well. I could release accurate words of knowledge (facts) and give words of wisdom (future) with precision. I was able to discern spirits and differentiate between God and the evil one. Surely, all of this added to my internal confusion and fed the identity conflict. I needed answers, "Was I an evangelist, a prophet, or a pastor?"

Consequently, as I began to read the Gospels, I instantly became cognitively captured. The Scriptures came alive as the Holy Spirit deposited evangelistic revelations into my spirit which internally set me ablaze…*forever*!

I saw Jesus as I had never seen Him before, as an evangelist. The more I studied Jesus, I noticed undeniable distinct Holy Spirit inspired characteristics about Him. To my amazement, I shared those exact, same characteristics!

My study of the Gospels from an evangelistic perspective was meticulous and exhaustive which took months. Countless hours of research were conducted during my study because I desired to learn as much as possible about the evangelist. The more I studied about the evangelist, it became indisputably obvious that I _was_ indeed an evangelist. Although I could genuinely flow and operate in prophetic realms and function as a pastor, my primary grace was that of an evangelist. Whew!

I lack words to accurately articulate the level relief I experienced with the revelation and acceptance of being an evangelist. I was liberated from an assumed yet false burden of being something I was not and trying to sit in a seat that I was not called nor anointed to occupy; that was both bitter and sweet.

Conversely, I felt a new burden called, "Fear-of-the-unknown." I embraced being an evangelist, because I finally had definition of _"who"_ I was and _"What"_ I was called to do. Both the "_who_" and the "_what_" were active ingredients burning in my soul and were mixing simultaneously which produced a hunger to be God's evangelist which ultimately produce something unprecedented within me.

For the first time in my ministry, I had clarity. It was clear in my spirit and resolved in my soul that I was an evangelist. That revelation fueled me and empowered me to be my authentic evangelistic self. For the first time in my

Christian life and possibly for the first time in my entire life, I was confident and secure.

Without hesitation, I announced my resignation as a pastor and because most of my family/friends were not interacting with me, I had uninterrupted time to study, prepare, and equip myself as an evangelist.

Studying the life and earthly ministry of Jesus and Philip the evangelist was my lifeline in that season. Looking back, had not God given me the assignment to study "The Evangelist" by investigating Jesus, I do not believe I would have survived that depressing season in my life. No pun intended but it was "The Word" which saved me...for a second time!

After I discovered what an evangelist looked like and received a clear definition of an evangelist, I concluded once again that I was indeed an evangelist! One would think I would have been ecstatic to finally discover not just my kingdom assignment but my identity; however, it was far from elation and exhilaration.

In transparency, the first time I proclaimed "I am an evangelist" after I resigned as a pastor, it felt odd. Honestly, there were times when it felt like I had been demoted. I challenged myself to understand why being an evangelist seemed less prestigious than a pastor in my own view. I had no legitimate philosophy for my feelings other than I placed greater value on certain ministry gifts and lesser value on other ministry gifts.

In other words, I walked in a degree of pride as a pastor that I did not walk in as an evangelist because *"I"* honored and esteemed the office of pastor more highly than the office of an evangelist. Therefore, as an evangelist, it felt like I had been demoted in the spirit which was fueled by the haughtiness and conceit of my own heart. Initially the demoted feeling made it difficult to fully, publicly embrace my title and role as an evangelist.

In addition, my "demoted" status was reinforced when I noticed the odd actions of some of my senior pastor friends. They changed their interactions with me when my title changed from pastor to evangelist. Paradoxically, I was not acknowledged as I had been in the past when I visited their church services i.e. I was not escorted to the front row as an evangelist like it was when I was a pastor, nor was I offered the microphone like in times past. Not that I needed those things, but it was oddly noticeable, felt strange, and was arduous to experience the obvious shifts in my pastor friends. I examined my own heart as well as the heart and motives of others; both were not good reflections.

As a result, feelings of rejection, offense, and victimization manifested in my soul and colored vivid images on the tapestry of my mind. Consequently, I resolved I had to be intentional about resisting ungodly, soulish feelings of rejection. I could not become offended by the reactions nor responses of others. Neither could I become a rejected, offended victim if I was going to succeed as a Christian and walk in my true calling as an evangelist. Therefore, I decided to keenly focus on being a Christian and learn how to execute my assignment in the earth as God's evangelist.

The more I studied and learned about "The Evangelist," I realized I had not been demoted but rather I had been promoted! It was a promotion because God trusted me to deliver the distinct message of salvation and deliverance which will miraculously draw people to Him; that was and still is an honor to be God's evangelist!

Once I discovered and fully embraced my God-given identity and assignment as an evangelist, I entered a new level of authoritative power against the kingdom of darkness. Unexplainable peace flooded my heart which also broke insecurity, insanity, intimidation, and instability off my life and ministry. Doors of opportunity sprung open, old relationship restored, and new relationships birthed as a direct result of my whole-hearted acceptance and obedience to my evangelistic assignment.

Conversely, I had to stop flirting with being anything other than an evangelist; multi-tasking in ministry proved to be a deadly distraction which prevented me from giving my full self to being developed into God's evangelist. Yes, I had to fully surrender the thought of being a pastor, a prophet, and other things I did quite well. I embraced that I was an evangelist, and all other gifts, talents, and ministry streams were to enhance my evangelistic call, but *not* place me in another office simply because I could flow in the prophetic or function as a pastor. Once that was settled, I was free to be, "Linda, the evangelist" and function as God created me without apology, hesitation, nor reservation.

I never thought accepting who I was in God would usher in streams upon streams of joy, peace and stability; and for that I am grateful!

My name is Linda D. Jernigan,
"I AM AN EVANGELIST!"

WORD TO THE EVANGELIST
"Our Time is *NOW!*"

It is duly-noted that you have been confused about your calling, over-looked, and even dishonored. You may have even become discouraged as you've witnessed a surge in prophetic ministry, as ministry to the evangelists is obsolete and seems unimportant; that has been frustrating to watch and painful to experience but, you are still without excuse!

Evangelist…ma'am/sir, this is your time! This is your hour to *"Go"* and gather the harvest by preaching the Gospel and making disciples. Do not wait another year, month, or week, because the harvest is ready and waiting for you to get into position and perform your kingdom assignment. Look at what Jesus said…

> *"Say not ye, there are yet four months*
> *and then cometh harvest? Behold, I say unto you,*
> *Lift up your eyes, and look on the fields:*
> *for they are white [ripe] to harvest."*
> John 4: 35 (KJV)

The dangerous, distraction of most evangelists is they feel unequipped and unprepared to do the work of an evangelist as exhorted by the Apostle Paul in 2 Timothy 4:5. Most evangelists wait and wait and wait because they are seeking and searching for patterns, blueprints, and models for evangelistic ministry. In the interim, precious viable time is squandered which will never be reclaimed. Most evangelistic ministry is swallowed up in procrastination and internal uncertainty.

At some point, evangelists must explore their own evangelistic journey by following the trail blazed by other evangelists. This can be accomplished by connecting with active successful evangelists who has a proven evangelistic record which speaks to your future destiny. In addition, read evangelistic books, watch evangelistic videos, subscribe to evangelistic channels, and enroll in evangelistic courses and classes for expanded development. For those on the uncharted, unprecedented path, you may have to become the model and blueprint for others to follow.

Evangelists should be trained and discipled by another evangelists. However, most of what evangelists need will manifest by personal, passionate pursuit displayed by seeking resources on their own. Listen, you must seek resources and converse with people who can equip you. You cannot be lazy! Be aggressive when it comes to your development as an evangelist. Invest time and money to learn your craft and calling. Again, you cannot be lazy!

Over the years, evangelists have lamented to me by confessing that "they do not know where to begin." This is understandable as the Bible have only a few reference Scriptures for the evangelists, and most evangelists have not had an evangelistic mentor, never been discipled, nor matriculated in evangelistic classes and trainings to equip them as they evolve in the evangelistic grace.

I must admit that training and equipping evangelists have been anemic in local churches, but the expectation for evangelists to produce measurable results have always been high. That is quite unfair and is the primary cause of ministry insecurity in most evangelists. How can evangelists be expected to produce when they have not been trained, equipped, empowered, nor have they been given resources (people and money) to ensure success?

For this reason, many evangelists have retreated inward and became silent while others abandoned the call of the evangelist but grabbed the title of a prophet to fit into religious circles for equipping, acceptance and comfort. Because evangelists felt unequipped, they became discouraged, and discouragement caused them to abandon their evangelistic call.

As an evangelist, there are steps you must take to initiate and take responsibility for your own ministry growth and development. Below are five suggestions to help activate you and get you moving.

1. **Read your Bible!** This is the most important thing you can do to equip yourself as an evangelist. The mysteries within the Bible will be unveiled as you read the Bible more and more. It's a Holy Spirit thing which will lather up in you as you stick with it. Read the Bible and keep reading the Bible. Never stop reading the Bible nor substitute the Bible for other readings. Whether you feel it or recognize it, when you read the Bible, it is being absorbed into your heart. You are learning, growing, and it *is* getting inside of the crevasses of

your soul. You will be able to recall it and share it, as you continue to read it. Do not stop, "Read your Bible!"

2. **Educate Yourself!** As you read the Bible, gain an understanding of Salvation. Educate yourself beyond the "Prayer of Salvation" and Romans 10:9-10. Study synonymous salvation terms like justification, redemption, reconciliation until you are comfortable, and have appropriate language with precise articulation mixed with Scriptures as your evidential support. This will build your confidence. As an evangelist, you must understand salvation and have the ability to talk about it and defend it in diverse environments and with diverse people groups. Give yourself six months to study Biblical salvation and increase your knowledge and language connected to salvation.

3. **Pray**! As you broaden your personal prayer time to include prayers for salvation in your family, the church, and the world, you will become more sensitive and more discerning to the spiritual needs of people. This will increase your evangelistic grace and give you deep spiritual insight into the lives of people despite what they verbally tell you. God will trust you with more information because you pray to Him concerning people, and not gossip with or about people.

4. **Share Jesus!** Start with the people you know i.e. family members, friends, coworkers and neighbors. Casually insert Jesus into conversations to gage if a person is connected to Jesus. If you determine they

are disconnected from Jesus, then strategically introduce Jesus to them as One who should be in their life.

5. **Build Connections!** Connect with someone who can disciple you as an evangelist and become engaged in an evangelistic community.

   A. **Disciple**: As an emerging evangelist, if you desire to be discipled, you will need to initiate the first step. Do not wait for someone to approach you because most likely that will not happen. You will need to be bold and humble yourself and ask to be discipled. By chance, if you cannot be discipled by the evangelist of your choice, then ask them for resources to build your evangelistic life i.e. book referrals and study materials. Likewise, inquire about conference information specifically for evangelists/preachers. Do not procrastinate and hope someone comes your way and grabs you up. No! Pursue it, and make it happen. You need to be discipled!

   B. **Evangelistic Community**: In 2020, I established an evangelistic community called, "The Evangelism Coalition." You can connect with us on Facebook or subscribe to our YouTube channel or our website, EvangelismCoalition.com. Our "Evangelism Coalition" community is a great place to start to connect with other evangelistic people. We offer classes and trainings and an environment where you can grow as an evangelist. Yes, you can be trained as an evangelist, gain information on how to conduct outreaches, and to be licensed and ordained through our organization (You do not have to leave your church). In fact, "The Evangelism Coalition" was established as an extended arm of church, but not to replace the local church. Our vision is to train and equip evangelists and send them back to gather their own harvest i.e. church, ministries, cities, and regions. Give us a look.

Jesus said, "Do not say you have four more months.' In other words, do not say you have more time, or you will do it later. Jesus said, "Lift up your eyes!" In other words, stop looking down-trodden and defeated…come alive and look up. Jesus wants to give you a new perspective on your calling as an evangelist. He wants you to be fruitful in this land of evangelism, but you must make the conscience decision to "Look up!" Be optimistic and allow the energy of the Holy Spirit to fuel your faith in this season. "Look up!"

As you look up, you will see culture and all the challenges that has occurred. As an evangelist, you can no longer walk around with your head down and ignore what is happening in the world. Jesus said, "Look on the fields." In other words, "Look at your family, look at your co-workers, look at your neighbors, look at the next generations, look at the politicians, look at America, and look at the world… you see that they *need* you to bring them some good news. Come on, evangelist! Look up and look around, you are necessary.

The wonderful thing about being an evangelist is you can fit into any sector of society! This is both intricate and complex which is a blessing and a challenge for evangelists. (1) It is a blessing because evangelists can slide into and fit into almost any environment and leave a deposit (2) This can be a challenge because it makes it difficult to place evangelists into a specific box or label them because they do many things well, with multiple interests and complimentary gifts and talents.

Evangelists are diverse and can be useful in several areas of ministry and have multiple careers. This innate ability comes with challenges because it makes it nearly impossible for evangelists to be placed in any one area for an extended period of time. As an evangelist you can enter politics and/or produce films. You can cook food as a career, sew clothes, and even sing songs. You can write books or novels and enter public service as a police officer, lawyer, doctor, educator, or social worker. Because the evangelistic grace is diverse, you can choose your career path and still be a productive evangelist in ministry.

Therefore, you are without excuse! Lift your eyes and look on the fields for they are white [ripe] to harvest. The question is, "Are you willing and ready to be deployed?"

*"The harvest truly is plenteous,
but the labourers are few:*

INTRODUCTION

Evangelists are needed! If you have any doubt, take a panoramic view of society i.e. terrorist attacks, record-setting school shootings, blatant "smash-and-grab" unconcealed robberies and thefts, fear-filled carjackings, celebrity and Christian suicides, debilitating depression, immeasurable poverty, perverse, polluted politics, and agonizing addictions to nearly everything which isn't nailed down, and you will see undeniable, irrefutable proof that society is screaming for evangelists! Culture's chaos is Kingdom coded language for the necessity of evangelists.

The pitiful yet pathetic truth is that most Christians do not understand evangelists. Therefore, they are oblivious to the collective, communal needs in society because of the absence and suppression of evangelists.

Evangelists are the bridge by which people travel to meet Jesus. With Jesus being "The Answer" to all cultural chaos and confusion, without Jesus society will become degenerate and digress into a dismal abyss, much like we are witnessing today.

Unfortunately, pastors are also uninformed to the horrific consequences the church and culture face because of missing and restrained evangelists. When evangelists are not permitted, equipped, and released to do the work of evangelists, the effect of that suppression reverberates throughout the entire world. Again, much like the cultural chaos we have in effect today.

Understand this, evangelists are necessary because…

(1) Evangelists carry the responsibility to preach the Gospel and introduce people to Jesus!

This is extremely important! Romans 10:14 says, "…how shall they hear without a preacher?"

The word preacher means, "One who herald divine truth, the gospel. Proclaim, publish."

In Ephesians 4:11, the title evangelist means, "a preacher of the gospel, bringer of good tidings."

Who does not want to hear good news? Evangelists are anointed and have a distinct talent to articulate the good news of the Gospel and release divine truth. Often, evangelists present the truth enmeshed in humor for easier consumption and digestion.

Without evangelists, society is robbed of the good news and lacks the impartation of divine verity that the evangelistic grace carries. In a world that is filled with error and deception, hurt and depression, confusion and bewilderment, it needs the mouthpiece of an evangelist that will announce uncompromised truths and bring good news into environments and situations where personal challenge, struggle, and despondency is dominant. When evangelists are empowered to execute their assignment, the overall results have been favorably impactful…as proof, look at the first Biblical record of an evangelist operating as an evangelist and notice the results.

"And many of the Samaritans of that city
believed on him [Jesus] for the saying
of the woman, which testified…"
John 4:39 (KJV)

That passage confirms that an entire city was impacted by one evangelist. The Samaritan woman who had a personal encounter with Jesus at Jacob's well evangelized an entire city. This occurred when the Samaritan woman shared her personal experience with others, that she had with Jesus. The Samaritan woman did not quote the entire Bible, nor preach a 3-point sermon but rather she simply shared her experience with Jesus, and it impacted an entire city.

"And many of the Samaritans of that city
believed on him [Jesus] for the saying of the woman,
which testified…"
John 4:39 (KJV)

Did you get that? Many in the City of Samaria believed in Jesus because the Samaritan woman shared, published, preached, proclaimed the good news of her personal encounter with Jesus. It works, evangelists. It worked back then, and it still works now. Share Jesus!

Evangelists have stories to tell, and they should share them with anyone who will listen! This should not be disdained nor resisted. Evangelists record life experiences, both good and bad, and are graced to share their experiences with the hope that listeners will be encouraged in Jesus. This is a God-given gift which should not be overlooked nor suppressed. Even when evangelists prophesy or exhort, it may include a personal story or a relevant encounter/testimony to brighten people's acceptance of Jesus. It is the evangelistic way which may not be the prophetic or the pastoral way, but it's the evangelistic way.

We can experience identical evangelistic results with entire cities and regions coming to Jesus because of the evangelistic grace if we identify, train, and _seriously release_ evangelists! I say, "_seriously release_" because in recent decades the release of evangelists has been nothing more than a horse and pony show. Much fanfare around elaborate ordination ceremonies with sumptuous prophetic words, but not a real _release_ with permission, authority, and ministry support to create and implement discipleship plans (teach, train, equip inside church), with follow-up systems to retain new members/visitors, and financial investments into evangelism/outreach endeavors. It was a good emotional ordination ceremony, but the actual _release_ evangelists need to operate as an evangelist falls short of the elaborate ceremony; for this reason, true evangelists are frustrated and flocked into other communities, primarily prophetic environments for validation and acceptance.

Most evangelists receive their ministerial license and remain seated in the pews until it's time to perform a function outside of the church. i.e. back to school, Thanksgiving, Christmas, nursing homes, prisons, youth homes, food/clothes distribution, etc. All of those are good endeavors and should be applauded and supported. However, Ephesians 4:11-12 clearly gives evangelists a mandate to (1) perfect (mature/develop) the saints (2) prepare believers for the work of ministry and (3) to edify (build up) the body of Christ, which are all done *inside* of the church. Evangelists are not just for outside work i.e. street preaching and outreaches. In addition, evangelists have a solid word from the Lord which should be allowed to perfect (mature) and edify (build up) believers who attends church.

Evangelists are spiritually discouraged because they are overlooked until church attendance numbers decrease or plateau, then pastors want to put a microphone in the evangelist's hand to excite the crowd to create momentum, solely to increase attendance. That's a hype-man or at best the job of a marketer.

Evangelists are Kingdom promoters, which is a spiritual assignment. Evangelists are not mere marketers to solely increase church numbers and improve church statistics. Evangelists are interested in issues which plagues people's soul, and they desire to disciple them into healthy solid resolutions. Evangelists are interested in transformations and not just seat-fillers in the congregation.

When matters of the soul are addressed in people, the healed person becomes a marketing billboard for a church. With that being said, there is no need to pressure evangelists to host event after event after event, conference after conference, nor create catchy church themes for the sole purpose of increasing (1) curiosity of the church (2) church visibility and (3) church attendance, if lives were being changed there. A transformed life is the greatest, most effective promotion a church need.

Although I am not opposed to marketing and strategic advertising, in addition to those, we must endorse and promote *"changed lives"* as the primary marketing strategy for church and ministry. When people see that lives are being changed and people become better under a particular church, people will connect because God will send them to receive the help He desires to give His children. Focus on "Changing Lives" and watch how quickly the ministry grows.

Again, evangelists have the potential to transform cities and impact regions because transformation is one of the manifestations of the evangelistic grace. Evangelists are graced with the ability to transform because of their heavy dependency on the free-flowing power of the Holy Spirit and the heavy reliance on the Word of God. Accordingly, the entire world could benefit by the identification, activation, and liberation of the evangelist.

It is my personal belief that many people in society and within churches are dangerously depressed, devoid of destiny, and their life's purpose is unidentified because evangelists are *NOT* bringing the good news of, "Jesus is *'the'* answer!" Some evangelists attempt to present Jesus as *"a"* answer to not offend culture. However, the good news of the Gospel is, "Jesus is *'the'* answer," for every problem, every challenge, and every impossibility… "Jesus is *'the'* answer!"

It is that message which brings liberation and transformation, and evangelists cannot be timid to declare the simple, absolute truth of, "Jesus is *'the'* answer." History testifies that when Jesus is presented as the unequivocal explicit answer, people respond, and their response is assured because people are searching for direct, unambiguous and unmistakable clear answers.

(2) Evangelists are Conduits of Joy!

Not only does people accept Jesus as their savior when evangelists preach and proclaim Jesus, they also bring joy into cities and regions as Acts 8:8 (KJV) declares about Philip, the evangelist.

"And there was great joy in that city."

Can you imagine an entire city filled with joy? Most cities in America are filled with crime, addiction (alcohol/drugs/pills/food), depression, sexual perversion and brokenness, political greed, hatred, poverty, and sickness and disease which restricts the joy experience. It is quite difficult to experience joy when you battle any of the aforementioned areas.

Everyone must understand, including evangelists that the evangelist can bring joy into every environment because evangelists present Jesus as *"the"* answer to crime, addiction/drugs, depression, sexual brokenness, political greed, hatred, poverty and sickness and disease. When Jesus is offered as *"the"* answer, that secretes hope into people and when hope enters, joy will soon follow.

Subsequently, where laws and lawmakers fail to discover long-term solutions through legislation and public policies, Jesus provide answers by transforming people's heart and upgrading their morality through His principles. This conversion release rivers of joy in individuals and reverberate throughout their sphere of influence. This is the good news evangelists bring which results in the swelling of joy in the heart. The oppressed one discovers joy, then their family and friends' experiences joy as they witness their loved one free from the bondages which once held them as captives. Evangelists brings joy!

When evangelists are present, there should be increased levels of joy and jubilation in the room. Evangelists are immersed in joy. Evangelists can be joyful even during times of personal stress, tests, and trials; and they can bring joy to others *during* those times.

Do not ask how it's done because most evangelists will confess, they cannot explain why they are infinitely joyful. It's congenital. Evangelists joy levels increase when they see others being filled with joy through their ministry, jokes, stories, acts of service, and anointing. It's a boomerang effect for evangelists, as they release joy, the joy bounces back onto them and they too are filled with the joy they released onto others.

In short, this is what evangelists looks like and how the evangelistic grace functions. God created evangelists because they must share the good news of the Gospel, and they cannot be sad and depressed when they execute their evangelistic assignment; that's not attractive nor magnetic. Evangelists must be a plumbline of joy in churches, cities, and regions…evangelists bring joy! With that being said, let's resolve that evangelists are necessary!

As you progress through this book, settle in your heart that evangelists are not dispensable superfluous inanimate objects in the church nor in the Kingdom of God. Evangelists are necessary because there is a dire, essential church and cultural need for evangelists, more now than ever before. God's response to the world's chaos is to send courageous fire-lit evangelists into the earth with the good news of the Gospel to dispense hope and elevate levels of joy as He saves and delivers His people. Evangelists cannot be cramped nor hindered by the church nor entangled in religious systems which will only suppress them.

The church must respond by *seriously* releasing evangelists and allow them to execute their evangelistic assignments without religious constraints nor in comparison to other ministry gifts. Once church leaders comprehend the revelation of autonomy of five-fold ministry gifts with the necessity of each office, then they will be more accepting of each gift, similarities and differences, knowing that all are needed.

It is my belief that we are in the genesis of evangelists being equipped, released, and accepted as evangelists. This shift in Kingdom culture is becoming more apparent to Christian leaders as both church attendance and spiritual health has declined. Currently, there is more interest in employing Biblical evangelists than it has been in recent times. This shift open opportunities to equip and deploy evangelists for evangelistic service, both inside and outside of the church.

As the uptick increases in volume and in favor of evangelists globally, let it be known that...

The Evangelists are Coming!

PART ONE

EVANGELIST: THE PERSON

Chapter One
~ Jesus and His Earthly Ministry ~

Is there a model or procedure manual for emerging evangelists to follow? Where are the examples and templates for evangelists, much like the models which preachers, apostles, and prophets have to assist them in their ministry development...where is this located for evangelists? Where is the evangelistic blueprint which communicates how evangelists are to execute their ministry assignment?

Those questions have been internally asked by every person who accepted the call of an evangelist. Those questions are common because there are minimal teachings, trainings, and development tracks in Christian churches available for evangelists. Teachings for pastors (shepherds) and teachers were already common. Both Christian and secular educational institutions for pastors and teachers are readily available for development and continued growth.

Recently there has been increased teachings and trainings available for apostles and prophets, but still very little for the evangelist. Of the five-fold ministry gifts mentioned in Ephesians 4:11, the office of the evangelist is the least recognized and the most misunderstood which caused evangelists to be the least received and under-utilized in most Christian churches.

To get a better understanding of the evangelist, I conducted an exhaustive Biblical study of "evangelist" and there were only three mentions of the word "Evangelist" in the Bible (KJV). That discovery alone further acerbated me, I said, "Only three Scriptures?"

From that frustration, I began to study the Gospels to take another in-depth look into Jesus. I frequently read the Gospels because I am always fascinated with Jesus. Here is what I discovered about Jesus, *The Evangelist* as I read the Gospels...

> *"And Jesus went about all Galilee, teaching in their synagogues, and preaching the gospel of the kingdom, and healing all manner of sickness and all manner of disease among the people."*
> Matthew 4:23-25 (KJV)

The first thing which jumped off the pages to me as I read this passage was something which would become quite significant to me in the future. Within that passage of Scriptures, I saw that Jesus gave us four areas of concentration which reads as a Messianic message to guide evangelists. It is our evangelistic model from The Master.

1. JESUS WENT ABOUT

In our modern-day vernacular, we identify one who "goes about" on a specific assignment as itinerant. According to Merriam-Webster Dictionary, the word itinerant means, "Traveling from place to place to work."

For evangelists, being permitted to "Go About" is the lifeline to both natural life and ministry life. It is dangerous and will soon be proven to be fatal to constrain and confine evangelists; that will prove to be catastrophic as evangelists need to "GO" and move around.

To constrain evangelists is similar to spiritual suffocation. True evangelists will manifest symptoms of claustrophobia and hyperventilate when constrained, constricted, or confined to a space. That's what it feels like to evangelists when they are given instructions to "fit in" to be like others and that does not work well for evangelists. Evangelists need space to move around, go about, and to be themselves. Evangelists need diversity and spontaneity.

In addition, evangelists need assignments. How they fulfill assignments may be eccentric and unorthodox, however evangelists will complete their assignments in excellence and with extreme precision because their heart is connected to their assignment. That's how evangelists roll.

In John 4:34 (KJV), Jesus made it crystal clear that His earthly focus was steered towards completing the assignment which His father sent Him accomplish.

"My meat is to do the will of him that sent me,
and to finish his work."

Jesus was on earth to *work*! He understood His assignment in the earth and was never confused about it despite what other religious people were doing or how they conducted themselves. Jesus worked and He *went about* in an effort complete His work assignment as John 17:4 (KJV) confirms.

"I have glorified thee on the earth:
*I have finished the **work** which thou gavest me to do."*

Therefore, Jesus Himself modeled what it means and what it looks like to be an evangelist on the "Go." Evangelists "Go About" (or travel) to do "Work" for the kingdom, which God assigned for evangelists to do.

2. TEACHING IN THEIR SYNAGOGUES

One of Jesus's purposes as He *went about* was to teach. Jesus taught the masses, the religious leaders of His day, and His disciples. He was called "Rabbi" (John 1:38, 1:49, 3:2, and 6:25) which means "Teacher." Jesus had a stellar reputation as a master teacher.

To the surprise of some, Jesus was NOT a senior pastor of a local church, but rather Jesus taught in *their* synagogues. This was an eye-opening revelation as I pondered my transition from a senior pastor into evangelist.

Not every preacher or teacher will become a senior pastor. Let that sink in. Jesus gave us permission to teach in *their* synagogues or in various venues. We do not have to have our own church or ministry, and we can be valuable and effective serving in someone's ministry.

As an evangelist, our goal or ambitious aspiration in ministry is not to become a senior pastor. Hear me clearly, everyone will not have their own church nor their own ministry. That thought is a modern-day trap which feeds rebellion and pride and it the primary cause for ministry failure.

However, evangelist must be empowered to continue to teach the Bible and proclaim the good news as opportunities are presented. Even if it means teaching in *their* synagogues or in other people's church, ministry and even in another religious institution. Evangelist can "GO" and teach in other places. It is part of their call.

To teach in *their* synagogues is to teach in unorthodox environments. Oftentimes, that will be in places or with people who oppose the Kingdom of God message. As evangelists, you cannot be content with applauses and amen's because you only go to friendly spaces. On the contrary, sometimes you should hear people gasp for air, and metaphorically see them "clutch their pearls."

In other words, sometimes your words and teachings should stun people. Why? Well, because the Gospel can be offensive when presented undiluted, especially when you teach Jesus's truth in *their* synagogues or churches and not just a personal place of comfort. When evangelists fully comprehend this concept, then they will be liberated to "Go About" and "Teach in *their* synagogues."

3. PREACHING: KINGDOM GOSPEL

John preached one message, "Repent." Jesus had a message too, *"The Gospel of the Kingdom."* From Matthew - John, Jesus mentioned the word "Kingdom" over one hundred times. Surely, Jesus was committed to the message He was sent to preach. In Jesus' day, there were philosophers who had different philosophies and ideologies. However, Jesus was assigned His message by Father God and He faithfully preached, *"The Gospel of the Kingdom."*

Jesus tailored His "Gospel of the Kingdom" message to be relevant to the issues of the day. Jesus spoke of taxation, infidelity, marriage, children, family, poverty, anger, retaliation, forgiveness, and service to humanity. However, Jesus did not abandon His Kingdom message nor did He "water-down" the message to make others feel comfortable. Rather Jesus consistently preached the uncompromised *"Gospel of the Kingdom."*

In my early preaching years, I opposed the message of salvation and deliverance because I wanted to be a popular preacher. I went to Bible college and wanted to be accepted as a prolific preacher and show off my preaching chops. I believed if I preached salvation and deliverance, I would not be a highly sought after preacher, nor have a busy preaching schedule as I desired. I naively thought I could choose what I preached because this was *my* ministry. Wrong!

Just as God gave Jesus a message and John a message, He gave me a message too. In fact, I believe God gives people their messages and assigns the lane they should occupy based on their gifts, personality, and what's needed to advance His Kingdom. God is the employer, and He fills positions based on what He needs at the time and in a particular place; that's what makes Him sovereign.

As a young preacher, that was not explained to me. As a result, I wasted time trying to carve my own path with my own desires and ambitions, based on what I thought would bring me ministry success. I failed miserably! Ministry success did not come until I surrendered my ministry ambitions and my definition of ministry success and exchanged it for God's path of ministry for me. I had to embrace the message of salvation and deliverance as my main entrée, with evangelism, prayer, and leadership as optional appetizers or desserts.

Just as Jesus, John, and myself had to embrace God's divine message assigned to us, all evangelists must know the specific message God gave them to preach. Once that message is discovered, preach all the juice out of it (if possible) and you will experience ministry success!

4. HEALING ALL SICKNESS AND DISEASE

In Jesus earthly ministry, He demonstrated that He did not agree with sickness! For this cause, He healed *ALL* manner of sickness and disease. When people were sick around Jesus, He healed them. Jesus healed people of sickness because in God's perfect will, He desires that none are sick. 3 John 2 (KJV) declares,

"Beloved, I wish above all things that thou mayest prosper and be in health, even as thy soul prosperth."

Jesus healed *ALL* manner of sickness and disease!

Healings, both physical and emotional healings were common normality's in Jesus' ministry. Jesus routinely healed and He healed every form of sickness and disease that was present in His era. Jesus proves to us that God's will is not for any to be sick nor diseased; this is why He healed. Jesus would NEVER do anything that Father God was not in agreement. In fact, Jesus said in John 5:19 (KJV),

*"...The Son can do nothing of himself,
but what he seeth the Father do:
for what things soever he doeth,
these also the Son likewise."*

Jesus was not on earth because He had an agenda He wanted to push. Jesus was on assignment from Father God (just as every evangelist), and He did exactly what God instructed Him to do. Therefore, if Jesus healed, it was because God instructed Him to heal. Subsequently, if God instructed Jesus to heal then surely, we are expected to heal too.

I am aware that there are Christians who oppose healing because they believe some sicknesses are God's will. They believe God will use sickness or disease as some sort of test of faith. Therefore, when they pray, they say things like, "Lord, if it be your will, heal Sis Lucy." The Bible supports that it is God's will for everyone to be healed of sickness and disease. This is one reason Jesus died…for every stripe that Jesus took on the cross, it was packed with potential to free us from sickness and disease. Before Jesus' crucifixion and resurrection, the prophet Isaiah prophesied…

> *"But he was wounded for our transgressions,*
> *he was bruised for our iniquities:*
> *the chastisement of our peace was upon him;*
> *and with his stripes we are healed."*
> Isaiah 53:5 (KJV)

Later, the Apostle Peter comes along in 1 Peter 2:24 (KJV) and says something similar as he reflected at the healing provisions afforded to us through Jesus's crucifixion, he declares…

> *"Who his own self bare our sins in his own body*
> *on the tree, that we, being dead to sins,*
> *should live unto righteousness:*

by whose stripes ye were healed."

Therefore, we need not pray those lame, faithless prayers! During Jesus' ministry He healed ALL manner of sickness and disease (Matthew 12:15, Matthew 14:14, Matthew 15:30, Matthew 21:14, Luke 4:40, and Luke 6:17) and we should heal too.

Much to my surprise, I saw Jesus as the original evangelist who created the template for evangelists to follow. This was shocking but refreshing as I prefer to follow Jesus's model over a man-made model anyway. However, it was still shocking to see Jesus as "The Evangelist" because I was not expecting that.

Again, Jesus (1) Went about (2) Taught in their synagogues (3) Preached the Gospel of the Kingdom and (4) Healed all sickness and diseases. The evangelistic example and model I secretly searched for in others and in other forms, I found in Jesus.

Jesus put the evangelistic model on display for our benefit. You want to know what you should do as an evangelist, do what Jesus did, "Go teach, preach, and heal." That's the blueprint Jesus left for us to follow as evangelists…that's the evangelistic model for the fulfillment of the evangelistic assignment; (1) Go (2) Teach (3) Preach and (4) Heal.

Chapter Two
~ Evangelist; The Person ~

While reading the Gospels, I noticed certain characteristics about Jesus when I studied His earthly ministry. Those characteristics were not just things which defined Christians, but they were evangelistic characteristics which directly defined me as an evangelist. Wow! The more I read about Jesus in the Gospels, my evangelistic identity became clear; more and more clear. That was what I had been in search of for years and I found it in the Gospels with Jesus.

In addition, an evangelistic model emerged from my study of the Scriptures, and it distinctly defined evangelistic characteristics of Jesus, Philip the evangelist, and even people like Evangelist Billy Graham, Evangelist Aimee Semple-McPherson, D.L Moody, and others who also displayed some of the same evangelistic characteristics which I studied; and many of them functioned in the earth as evangelists too.

It has been the absence of evangelistic definition which caused the under-development of evangelists. The result of that is minimal evangelistic fruit in most Christian churches and communities. When there aren't clear-cut definitions and Bible-based models for people to follow, it leaves the door open for the devil to deceptively define and create a false identity. This explains why evangelists desire to be prophets, apostles, pastors, and teachers because other offices have clear definitions of their calling and an explainable assignment which is easily identified.

Most evangelists are given a bullhorn, a hand full of informative tracks, a community outreach to promote the church, and escorted to the door with instructions to go "win the lost" without proper ministry education, ministry identification, nor ministry revelation about *"who"* they are as an evangelist and *"what"* they are being sent to accomplish.

Ultimately, under the indecorously identified evangelists very few people get saved and the church does not grow numerically nor in spiritual health. Why? Commonly the person who was identified as the church evangelist and placed over evangelism is not an evangelist at all!

Just because a person may be an energetic extrovert who loves interacting with people, talking about Jesus and salvation, adores being outside, and attends church regularly does not qualify them as an evangelist. NO! Let's be clear that an evangelist has distinguished traits which were instituted by Jesus and is the inheritance of evangelists.

To further damage the office of the evangelist, there are authentic evangelists working in other offices, primarily masquerading as prophets. It is dangerous to have evangelists functioning and identifying as a prophet as their primary gift. Although evangelists can flow in-and-out of other ministry gifts (they need to easily access any ministry's gift grace as they stand to snatch people out of hell), evangelists should not be ordained in other offices as their primary ministry gift. Consider yourself warned if you mislabel, misidentify, and misplace evangelists because you will regret it! Chaos and confusion will be the order of the day in your church.

Evangelists have their own characteristics, and the evangelistic grace works best in an environment where they can be their unique evangelistic self; and that evangelistic grace is quite distinctive from other ministry graces. One consistent thing about an evangelist is they will consistently be inconsistent without proper oversight to help them manage their evangelistic characteristics.

I do not proclaim that this is an exhaustive list to define evangelists but surely this will help identify most evangelists. It is my prayer that the list below will assist in identifying evangelists around the globe for the purpose of properly releasing them to gather the harvest which is currently ripe for the picking. The below list is not designed to restrict nor confine evangelists but rather this is to provide definition for clarity and unity among evangelists. We have an obligation to define, identify, and release evangelists into their office, give them permission to be evangelists, offer our support, and provide resources (money and people) for them to be successful. This is about evangelistic freedom!

The model I employ to identify evangelists is based on characteristics Jesus outlined in the Gospels during His earthly ministry. Most evangelists will identify and relate to many of the characteristics listed below. Some of the characteristics will be in the infancy stage while others will be more refined and easier to see.

~ HUMAN ~

"In the beginning was the Word (Jesus), and the Word (Jesus) was with God, and the Word (Jesus) was God. And the Word (Jesus) was made flesh (Human)..."
John 1:1, 14a (KJV)

Jesus was **HUMAN**! Yes, Jesus is God, but He was also human during His earthly ministry. However, Jesus was a flawless human. In contrast to Jesus, today's evangelists are humans who are indeed flawed. For those who believe they are flawless, the Bible says they are deceived.

"If we say that we have no sin,
we deceive ourselves, and the truth is not in us.
If we say that we have not sinned,
we make him a liar, and his word is not in us."
1 John 1:8, 10 (KJV)

Therefore, one of the first identifiable characteristics of an evangelist is, **HUMAN**. It sounds simple to say that evangelists are human but there are some who believe animals are evangelistic too. Although that seems interesting, be informed that evangelists preach the Gospel message of salvation and deliverance through Jesus Christ. It is yet to be seen or better yet heard where dogs, cats, birds, lions, bears or any other animal preach the Gospel message without the assistance of AI or another form of artificial technology. Therefore, animals cannot be evangelists because evangelists are human with the ability to preach the Gospel, which animals cannot do.

Human Antithesis: Evangelist are flawed! Every evangelist needs to hear they are not perfect. Because much of their time is spent discussing a perfect Gospel, evangelists must be reminded they are human and imperfectly flawed.

After preaching a perfect Gospel and living righteous for an extended period of time, evangelists must be careful and resist the temptation of becoming self-righteous. In self-righteousness, an evangelist will forget that they too are human with flaws and will lose sensitivity, compassion, and empathy for other people's process in their life's journey.

~ ITINERANT ~

Jesus was **ITINERANT**! Itinerant means "to travel from place to place for work" and Jesus went about preaching and teaching in their synagogues (Matthew 4:23), modeling itinerancy. Just as Jesus, the itinerant evangelist is one who will *go about*.

Most evangelists will enjoy traveling from place-to-place, city-to-city, town-to-town, state-to-state, country-to-country, and even event-to-event to share the Gospel message. Evangelists enjoy spontaneous, unplanned pick-up-and-go assignments! New places, new people, and new experiences is how most evangelists thrive and keep their fire burning.

Therefore, the itinerant nature of an evangelist must be respected and given space to express itself. Evangelists will diligently seek out places to go to assist others, especially with community endeavors and natural disasters i.e. Hurricanes, tornados, floods, and fires are pleasantly embraced opportunities for evangelists to serve and assist people who needs love and compassion. Like firemen, evangelists run into situations that others run away from.

Because of the evangelist's itinerant nature, their calendar can be filled with service commitments daily. Those commitments vary in communal needs and are often diverse assignments with diverse people groups. Evangelists can manage a daily schedule of service for weeks, and even months, without taking a day off. For this reason, evangelists need keen oversight i.e. supervisors, mentors, pastors, preferably apostolic pastors who can steward their evangelistic itinerant grace properly; especially if they are a novice, they will need ardent oversight to avoid burnout and waste.

Let's look at a sponge. A sponge soaks up liquids and releases that liquid when squeezed; that's similar to the itinerant evangelist. If the evangelist is connected to a ministry where they are fed a proper spiritual diet, and they are permitted to release what they personally soaked i.e. learned, studied, and consumed. The evangelist will be highly effective in their assignments. Like a sponge, they soak up the liquids and then release what was soaked into them.

However, if an evangelist is in an environment where they cannot express their itinerant nature by "going-and-doing," they will soon dry up. Just like a dry sponge, the restricted evangelist will eventually become hard and brittle and what they release will come from a hard, bitter place in their soul. This occurs because the restrictions on "going-and-doing" dried up their itinerant nature. Like an unused sponge, over time the evangelist became hard and brittle, due to being idle. They are unable to soak anything positive into them and become toxic to people.

When that happens, the dry evangelist's negativity will be clearly visible to everyone. They will become cynical complainers who are difficult to connect with, serve with, and unify with others. Sometimes, if it's caught early enough, something as simple as allow the dry evangelist to teach a small group, a Bible study, preach a sermon, or be given a new "*important*" assignment can be the antidote. Surely, an evangelist cannot do everything they desire, however room must be given for them to live out their God-given itinerant characteristic. Evangelists are itinerant!

Itinerant Antithesis: Evangelist can appear to be unstable because often they do not have longevity in their life, including a career or a church home. Evangelists' itinerant nature will prompt them to make sudden moves and quick changes; some of which can have long-lasting, negative results. Therefore, evangelists should keep their itinerant grace, but they must guard against being impulsive which leads to self-destruction.

Personally, my itinerant nature has cost me a great deal of pain throughout my life. I have impulsively without notice, nor for any good reason quit jobs, quit school, changed churches, closed businesses, dismantled teams, left relationships, spent money recklessly, and made unhealthy commitments and alliances. In my immaturity, I did not understand why I did things that way. I felt it strong in my spirit, so I instantly pulled the trigger. Therefore, to negate personal responsibility, I concluded that God was leading me, so I obeyed Him, and my 2nd excuse was, "This is how God made me so deal with it." Pure rebellion!

Well, God did create evangelists with an itinerant nature but according to Proverbs 10:22, "God's blessing was designed to make us rich (add value to our life) and not bring sorrow with it." Therefore, God has a way for us to express our itinerant nature without being destructive to ourselves or others.

It took me years to learn how to manage my itinerant nature so that it could be a blessing to my life and not be an instrument of satan to destroy my life and negatively impact my ministry. Hear this, simply because our gifts come from God, they must be stewarded properly and operate under the guidance of the Holy Spirit, while being submitted to someone else who have the authority to advise and give another perspective for consideration.

Consequently, I had to evict "impulsiveness" out of my soul. Without losing the ability to be flexible and to shift as the Holy Spirit leads, I had to acknowledge the dangers in being impulsive and making sudden emotional moves. To manage the itinerant part of me required accountability and "wise ropes." This means I gave others greater than myself permission to inspect me and use the "wise ropes" given to them through accountability and submission to "pull me in" when necessary.

To protect me against impulsiveness, I initiated a 48-hour rule which meant I would not make a final decision for 48-hours. This allowed the emotional wave to pass over and then I could think clearer without being emotionally stimulated. The 48-hour rule also applied to spending money, taking trips, responding to emails/texts, and agreeing to ministry assignments. "Wise Ropes" saved me innumerable times from hanging myself with dumb ropes connected to impulsiveness.

As an itinerant evangelist, it was imperative that I remained stable in my emotions with both good and bad emotions as emotional decisions can be costly. Simply having stabilized emotions brought a sobriety which destroyed the destructive powers of impulsiveness. As a result, I enjoy being itinerant (flexible, easy to shift). However, I most enjoy the blessings of itinerancy without experiencing the devastation of being unstable and impulsive which kept me on a constant course of correction and starting over and over and over again; continual restarts delayed my progression in life and ministry productivity.

~ DIRECT ~

Jesus was **DIRECT**! Because Jesus was **DIRECT**, He modeled how to be **DIRECT** and call a spade a spade.

I am alarmed by the need for Christians to sugar-coat their words to make them pleasant to all listeners. Most times, people do not receive a watered-down Gospel. They are looking for a strong, **DIRECT** leader who will tell them the truth and call things like they should be. Jesus showed us this when He called things as they were...he called a spade a spade when he called Herod a fox (Luke 13:32); a thief a thief when He called satan a thief (John 10:10), a liar a liar when He called satan a liar and the father of lies (John 8:44), and a hypocrite a hypocrite when He called the Scribes and Pharisees hypocrites (Matthew

23:13).   Jesus was **DIRECT** and called it exactly how He saw it to be. No sugar added!

If there is an evangelistic characteristic that will get evangelists in trouble today, I declare before you that being **DIRECT** is #1 on the list!

DIRECT evangelists are the most ostracized people walking the earth today because society lives in the gray area aka "politically correct." This perspective has hardened society against simple plain, black and white truth. Society have been lied to and deceived for so long that the truth is offensive. Because of this, it has become difficult for most people to appreciate someone who talks *directly* to them and gives unfiltered truth.

However, most evangelists thrive best in a clear, direct environment. If you ask an evangelist if they like blue, they will answer either "Yes or No." On the other hand, if you ask someone other than an evangelist, if they like blue, they may respond, "Well, it depends on what shade of blue…light blue or dark blue?" Evangelists like to get to the point and call things as they are seen. This is not to say that evangelists are always correct, but being **DIRECT** is an innate attribute of most authentic evangelists.

Equally important, evangelists should not be rude nor verbally abusive. There is a difference between being direct vs. being rude.   Being direct does not give evangelists permission to be reckless with their words, nor talk condescending to people. In fact, evangelists are to use their words to build people up and empower them by pointing them directly to Jesus.

My perspective is that God wired evangelists with a direct, matter-of-fact tongue so they will never convolute the message of salvation and deliverance. Certain things like salvation requirements can never get white-washed over with compromising politically correct language. Evangelists must be emphatic and direct about (1) Jesus is the ONLY way to God and (2) Salvation is freely given and is obtained by a verbal confessional invitation to Jesus and belief in the heart. (John 14:6, Romans 10:9-10)

If your best friend asked, "Will my mother go to hell because she does not believe in Jesus, nor has she invited Him into her heart, even though she's a good person?" The average person would have difficulty saying, "Yes, that is exactly what the Bible indicates." The average person will wiggle and bend to find a way to agree that their best friend's mom will escape hell, even if she never invites Jesus into her heart.

Most people will be unable to give their friend the direct truth because they would not want to hurt their friend's feeling nor make them angry. An evangelist must directly inform their best friend, without convoluted vague language that their mom is in danger of going to hell, if she continues to refuse Jesus. However, the evangelist will jump on the opportunity to encourage both the friend and their mom to invite Jesus into their hearts and that will resolve the hell issue and place her in heaven with Jesus for eternity.

For that very cause, the message of salvation and deliverance was trusted to the evangelist. God knew exactly who was needed to preach and teach the salvation message to a lost, dying, confused, rebellious world...He put the Gospel in the mouth of an uncompromising, unapologetic, **DIRECT** evangelists!

The problem is most people do not have a revelation of the evangelist. Therefore, when they encounter one who will speak **DIRECT** truth, they mislabel them as rude, harsh, brutal, opinionated, and controversial. When all that happened was, they encountered an authentic evangelist, who is **DIRECT** and cannot swim in the gray "make-me-feel-good, politically correct" pool.

Direct Antithesis: With a direct innate attribute, evangelists must guard against being insensitive. I have made some of my biggest blunders, not because I was wrong, but because I was not sensitive nor compassionate while being direct. Even with having a direct nature, evangelists are not exempt from being sensitive, compassionate listeners who are led by the Holy Spirit.

To increase sensitivity, compassion, and be preserved, evangelists should employ discretion as Proverbs 2:11 (KJV) says,

> *"Discretion will preserve you;*
> *understanding will keep you."*

Discretion will preserve (keep safe and protected) and help avoid unnecessary perils which mouth diarrhea (talking too much without thinking) can escort into your life and ministry. Evangelists need discretion to help protect them from themselves and the impulsiveness to share their thoughts and/or give an opinion. Discretion will help you keep quiet.

Discretion, "to judge wisely and objectively" is our working definition. When I have blundered with being direct, it was because I did not use discretion nor gained understanding of a situation before I spoke. When using discretion, it will inject sensitivity without diluting a direct response.

As evangelists learn to manage the **DIRECT** nature God gave to assist in the delivery of the Gospel message, evangelists must also be certain that they utilize other tools such as discretion before they speak.

Always assess and thoroughly measure situations first. Afterwards, gather facts by checking for valid information. Lastly, pray and ask God for the appropriate response. Be aware that quite often, the appropriate response is "NO" response at all. I've discovered that a verbal response is rarely required immediately.

Dear friend, discretion will give you time to collect your thoughts and develop a position. It will give you needed time to lather up compassion needed to release the best verbal response; a direct, yet compassionate response. Do not be eager to speak nor give your opinion but rather give yourself time to process all the information you have received. This small step will protect you from saying the wrong thing, even though you have the right intentions; even with right intentions, the hurt is the same. It is okay to pause for a minute to activate discretion before you speak a direct truth.

~ JOYFUL ~

Jesus was **JOYFUL**! When one look at Jesus's earthly ministry, it will be evident that after people encountered Him, they left with joy in their hearts and a thankful attitude for their encounter with Jesus; and they shared their experiences with others. (John 4:28-30, Luke 17:14-16).

Evangelists are **JOYFUL** too! This may be why evangelist can be the "Life" of the party, loudly laugh and have fun, participate in community outreaches and events, and do it all without murmuring and complaining. Evangelists are joyful and will inject joy into any environment!

It's the joyful, fun attribute of an evangelist that attracts people to them and gives evangelists the opportunity to share the Gospel with diverse people groups because joy makes them relatable.

The joy which evangelists displays, opens doors for them which a social media profile, a mere business card or website cannot do. People love to be around people who lives in joy, especially when there is much darkness, sadness, and despair in the world. Joyfulness is a characteristic which Jesus displayed (John 15:11) and Philip the evangelist modeled as well…

"Then Philip went down to the city of Samaria,

and preached Christ unto them. And the people with one
accord gave heed unto those things
which Philip spake, hearing and seeing the
miracles which he did. For unclean spirits,
crying with loud voice, came out of many that
were possessed with them: and many taken
with palsies, and that were lame, were healed.
*And there was great **JOY** in that city."*
Acts 8:5-8 (KJV)

Evangelists brings joy! Philip, the *evangelist*
brought **JOY** to an entire city…WOW!

Because evangelists have a God-given joyful
personality, when you're in the presence of an evangelist,
you will laugh and laugh even more. Evangelists share
amazing stories and tell side-splitting jokes which
commands joy to enter. An evangelist will change the
temperature in a room from dry and stale into bursts of
laughter simply because of the joy which resides in the
heart of the evangelist. Evangelists can shift an atmosphere
with their mere presence which oozes joy.

In recent years, I have become incredibly
comfortable with my joyful nature. I now include
storytelling and jokes into my messages and teachings. Joy
is like my wallet…I will not leave home without it. This
has worked well in building ministry and professional
relationships. My joyful nature is an evangelistic asset, and
it benefits my ministry.

As a deliverance minister, I speak on difficult
topics. Small doses of humor allow the thickness of the
message to be digested smoothly. Keep in mind that I
don't dilute my messages to appease people, but rather I

simply allow joy to escort the message into the depths of the soul uninterrupted by offense.

Subsequently, I have seen record-setting positive responses to my teachings and messages, since I added joy as one of my presentation ingredients. People remember and apply the lessons taught because they did not choke on the substance of the message because it was too thick. Joy made the message smooth and took it where it needed to go without resistance; that recipe has proven to work well for my listeners.

As a result, people feel comfortable with me and my ministry. They share the depths of their soul and most embarrassing truths with me. They feel safe and believe I understand them because I share personal embarrassing moments and speak on tough topics during my presentations. Because it is handled delicately, laced with a dose humor which causes them to relax, they then without hesitation experience the full benefits of joy. Being joyful builds trust which allows me to tackle bigger issues with people because of the safety net joy provides. Remember, a merry heart (laughter) is like a good medicine (Proverbs 17:22). Joy will do the hard work, when used properly.

With that being said, the mean person who have a difficult time engaging others is *not* an evangelist. Evangelists are not mean, rude, nor hard to get along with. Evangelists are fun and loving but are hard-core with the Gospel. They are 'chill' in most other areas which does not violate God's principles.

In addition, evangelists will be seen with a crowd. Why? Because the joy they carry attracts people to them and it is okay. It is the job of the evangelist to manage this and point people to Jesus which prevents idolization. However, insecure pastors and ministry leaders will be intimidated by this. It will appear that members of the congregation will like the evangelist more than the senior leaders. Insecure leaders will become alarmed that the evangelist will "steal" their members.

Fear of being labeled as a "member thief" hindered me for years as I did not want to appear to be one who was 'after' members of another church or ministry. Recently I became free of that thought and realized that that is the problem of the insecure pastor or leader and not my burden. I made the decision to interact, befriend, and receive every person within my sphere of influence to infect them with the joy of the Gospel. If a pastor or leader have a problem with that then they must take it to Jesus. Miss me with that insecure drama!

When evangelists have people, they have influence, and evangelists should have influence with people. This allows the evangelist to teach and disciple in an effective manner and confirms their calling as an evangelist. People want to be around and connect with a joyful evangelist and it's okay. This is because of the joy that evangelists release into the lives of people…the joy is the main attraction, and it allows the evangelist to share the Gospel, equip, and empower people into the Kingdom. Evangelists are joyful!

Joyful Antithesis: Joyful evangelist can also be playful and being playful resembles immaturity. Evangelists can be playful during inappropriate moments which makes them appear to be immature by others. Therefore, evangelist must monitor their jokes (types and timing) to ensure they are not offensive and as a result hinder people's acceptance of their ministry.

~ MAGNETIC ~

Evangelists are magnetic! Being magnetic is a loving, kind, innate trait dispersed by God with the intent to gather. God used love and kindness to magnetically draw us to Him and He gave love and kindness to us to draw others into the kingdom.

> *"...therefore with lovingkindness*
> *have I drawn thee."*
> Jeremiah 31:3 (KJV)

The American Standard Dictionary defines magnetic as, "Possessing an extraordinary ability to attract." It is synonymous with charisma and should be an asset to the ministry of evangelists.

People are magnetically drawn to evangelistic people and that is a great attribute to possess as a minister of the Gospel. When people are drawn to you, it deflates resistance and opens the grace to minister which makes the job of an evangelist much easier.

One thing I've discovered is that evangelists are magnetic because they are relatable. Their spotted, checkered past, and bad decisions infused evangelists with a deep well of empathy for others. Evangelists cautiously reserves judgment and criticism of people and aims it at the devil. Evangelists employ love, kindness, and understanding when dealing with people...all people. This makes evangelists relatable and draws people to them. Not only are people magnetically drawn to evangelists, but they will open up and share the intimate, secret parts of their life because they feel safe when they believe someone can relate to them and understand their experiences.

The uncommon part about that is people will also share the embarrassing details of their life…during the first meeting! People have said to me that they aren't sure why they told me all their personal business in our initial meeting. I hope it was because they were magnetically drawn to the God in me which caused them to feel safe.

In addition, an evangelist's joyful personality is often accompanied by a warm smile. The warm soft smile magnetically draws people as well. It gives the evangelist the ability to disarm people they've attracted and eventually they are able to gather them and bring them in closer. An evangelist's smile and joyful disposition becomes magnetically infectious. People love to sit at the evangelist's table and be in their presence. The magnetic attribute of an evangelist draws people and can be a benefactor as they share the Gospel of Jesus.

Magnetic Antithesis: People have the tendency to cling to the evangelist because of their magnetic personality. Therefore, evangelists must be focused to ensure they are not leading people to themselves but rather guide people to Jesus. The way to avoid that would be to habitually encourage people to read their Bible and become more acquainted with God for themselves. This should insulate the evangelist from becoming a god to people and the people from being easily deceived or manipulated by the evangelist. When the evangelist points people to Jesus, this helps people grow spiritually and avoid idolatry by becoming intoxicated with the evangelist.

~ SOLUTIONIST ~

If you want to agitate an evangelist, bring them a problem which you do not want a solution. That will cause an insurmountable amount of internal anguish for the evangelist because evangelists are *SOLUTIONIST*!

It annoys and disturbs the peace of an evangelist to talk about problem after problem after problem without working towards a solution. When this occurs, you will notice the evangelist will lose interest in the conversation, job, or project. If you want to keep things as they were, in regular formation, do not engage an evangelist in the process. However, if you desire answers, a resolution, and a solution, an evangelist is one of the people you should have on the team or even to lead the team.

According to the American Standard Dictionary, a solutionist is, "A solver of problems." It is imperative to understand that some people will think to solve problems and not just listen to problems. Evangelists are some of the people who are in the business of solving problems. The main problem evangelists contend with is people who are not connected to Jesus and risk going to hell by living a life of wickedness. Evangelists widely shares the Gospel of Jesus as the solution to all life's issues.

Being a *SOLUTIONIST* is an evangelistic characteristic demonstrated by Jesus, the Chief Evangelist. Jesus solved problems and resolved issues throughout His earthly ministry. In fact, Jesus' entire ministry was about bringing solutions to people which religious leaders either ignored, did not have the knowledge, power, nor ability to solve.

"And, behold, there cometh <u>one of the rulers of the synagogue</u>, Jairus by name; and when he saw him, he fell at his feet (23) And besought him greatly, saying, My little daughter lieth at the point of death: I pray thee, come and lay thy hands on her, that she may be healed; and she shall live."
Mark 5:22-23 (KJV)

According to this passage, Jairus was a religious ruler (leader) in the synagogue. Jairus had an understanding about healing through the laying on of hands, this is why he made a healing request of Jesus. In addition, Jairus also knew his daughter had a problem which he himself could not solve, even though he was a religious leader who served in the temple.

Therefore, Jairus sought Jesus because Jesus was a **SOLUTIONIST,** and Jairus knew Jesus would resolve the issue. Resolving issues was Jesus's reputation because He performed miracles and manifested solutions by: healing sick bodies, fed the hungry, extracted demons from people's souls, opened blind eyes, unstopped deaf ears, and even raised the dead. Jesus was a solutionist who solved many other problems before, and people knew this about Him. This is why Jairus had faith in Jesus' ability to solve the issue with his daughter, to heal her body and save her life; and Jesus did just that.

"And he cometh to the house of the ruler of the synagogue, and seeth the tumult, and them that wept and wailed greatly. (39) And when he was come in, he saith unto them, Why make ye this ado, and weep? The damsel is not dead, but sleepeth. (40) And they laughed him to scorn. But when he had put them all out, he taketh the father and the mother of the damsel, and them that were with him, and entereth in where the damsel was lying. (41) and he took the damsel by the hand, and said unto her, Talitha cumi; which is, being interpreted, Damsel, I say unto thee, arise (42) And straightway the damsel arose, and walked..."
Mark 5:38-42 (KJV)

Evangelist must be aware that solutionists work in unorthodox ways and people will laugh and mock them. It comes with the role of being a solutionist. For this reason, most people cannot operate as a solutionist nor solve problems. Most people are too enamored by what people think about them, so they reside on the street of "mediocrity" and remain on the "average" path to remain unified with the majority who don't have the courage to bring solutions.

Jesus walked into the ruler's house and said, "Stop all the crying, she's not dead but only sleeping." The people, the "regular" people who only see problems, laughed him to scorn. They mocked him and made fun of Him, when He was the *only* one with the answers and the solution.

Christians today would have gotten offended and caught up in their feelings and probably left God because people laughed at them. However, Jesus gave an example of how we should respond...produce results! People cannot argue, dispute, or deny authentic results. Therefore,

Jesus stayed focused and put them all out so he could solve the problem which He was called into the house to do!

Jesus knew who He was and what He could do. It was Jesus's proven record of results to solve problems which is why the ruler sought Him. The people who laughed at Him was not the people who hired Him, nor could they make or break His effectiveness, so Jesus got rid of them. He put *all* of them out! When Jesus put them out, then He was able to resolve the problem; heal the girl so she could live.

As a **SOLUTIONIST**, there will be times when you will need to solve problems or resolve an issue with a minimal audience. That is okay because you want results and solutions. You are not in a popularity contest nor are you working for the doubters and haters. You are hired by God to solve problems and resolve issues. This is a characteristic of evangelists, displayed by Jesus. Evangelists are **SOLUTIONIST**!

Solutionist Antithesis: Evangelists must be aware of the soulish seduction to resolve issues and solve problems which God has not assigned you to engage. This practice will burn you out quickly and positive results will be rare and few; that will bring discouragement.

Solutionists are not police who must respond every time someone has an emergency. Not! Rather, solutionists are wise, spirit led people who model Jesus. Jesus said He does and say what the Father tells Him to do and say (John 5:19). Jesus did not blindly nor emotionally walk into situations and just start working from His emotions. Jesus was clear-eyed and level-headed even at the wedding in Cana when His mom asked Him to solve a problem. Jesus told his mom that His time had not yet come (John2:4).

Remember, you are not the savior of your family, friends, church, nor the savior of the world. Jesus is the Savior for everyone who choses Him. If you attempt to step in His place and save the world, you will soon discover that it will be you who will need to be rescued from burnout and fatigue because you neglected yourself, your body, your finances, and your emotional health while trying to save others.

Evangelists are solutionist; however, wisdom is the principle thing. Always use wisdom (gather factual information) before joining in, taking a position, connecting with a situation or giving your support. Solve the problem, do not become part of the problem.

~ INQUISITIVE ~

Evangelists are **INQUISITIVE**! Evangelists will ask question after question after question and relentlessly interrogate a situation until they have a satisfactory understanding. Again, evangelists inherited that from Jesus, the Chief Evangelist. Jesus repeatedly asked His disciples questions.

"When Jesus came into the coast of Caesarea Philippi,
he asked his disciples, saying
Whom do men say that I the son of man am?"
Matthew 16:13, Mark 8:27, Luke 9:18 (KJV)

"He saith unto them, But whom say ye that I am?"
Matthew 16:15, Mark 8:29, Luke 9:20 (KJV)

Jesus asked His disciples questions to gage their understanding on various topics. In the above passage, Jesus asked questions about what people was saying about Him and what His disciples thought about Him after hearing what people said about Him.

Unlike Jesus who knew everything, evangelists ask questions to discover new information and to determine their position and response. Just like Jesus, (1) we must ask questions to know what is being said and (2) what is being said about us. People's opinion should not dictate our responses, but we should be aware of our name and reputation. One way to discover that is to ask questions.

The amazing thing about being inquisitive is that you have the emotional balance to evaluate each situation based on the facts and information presented. It takes a balanced, emotionally stable person to ask questions and to think critically before taking a position or releasing a response.

In America's political climate, being inquisitive is a lost, antiquated skill. Most people blindly and loosely agree with the people who shares their same political affiliation title without properly vetting or being inquisitive by asking important questions. Simply because a person claims to be a Democrat, or a Republican does not justify your agreement with them. It is your responsibility to be inquisitive and ask questions to ensure your beliefs and values are aligned.

If that is true in politics, surely that is true and must be the standard in church. Simply because a person says they are a Christian does not mean they believe and follow the teachings of Jesus Christ and apply them to their lives. What I have discovered, most professed Christians are merely members of a church and are not Christians. Therefore, when you as an evangelist encounter someone who is a professed Christian, it is within your range of authority to be inquisitive and ask questions to determine if they are Christians or are they simply church attendees.

If you determine through their answers that they are only church attendees, then you should attempt to move them into an authentic relationship with Jesus. However, you will never confidently know if you don't ask the appropriate questions.

Hear me clearly! Be inquisitive and ask questions so you can accurately determine your position and create a balanced, sober response. Evangelists are *INQUISITIVE!*

Inquisitive Antithesis: Nosey! Busy-body! Those are labels people will place on inquisitive evangelists because they ask questions.

People are shallow which makes inquisitive people seem nosey and deep. In other words, shallow people are uncomfortable with inquisitive people because inquisitive people are not easily fooled by a fast, quick talker. Nor is an inquisitive evangelist deceived by charismatic charm or amusement ministry tactics but rather they will soberly ask questions. An inquisitive evangelist will ask questions of everyone in the room to determine facts, no one is safe around an inquisitive evangelist.

An inquisitive evangelist will go beyond what has been said and ask questions about what was not stated and probe into *why* it was omitted. Inquisitive people hear differently from most other people. They can detect lies, exaggerations and hyperbolic language quicker than others. However, evangelists are not turned off by it, in fact it actually intrigues them and makes them want to hear more to learn how people arrived at their conclusions. For these reasons, inquisitive evangelists appear to be difficult or just plain nosey.

Lastly, as an evangelist, be certain the questions you ask are relevant to the topic at hand and the information is needed to help make a determination. Do not phish for information, just to be "in-the-know." Even as an inquisitive evangelist, there must be a standard of informational integrity which excludes gossip. Unnecessary information bends towards gossip and you must remain free of gossip. Only ask necessary, needed questions to formulate the appropriate response.

~ TEACHER ~

Jesus was known as the master **TEACHER**!

*"The same come to Jesus by night,
and said unto him, Rabbi (Master),
we know that thou art a teacher come from God:..."*
John 3:2 (KJV)

- 73 -

When Nicodemus addressed Jesus as "Rabbi," he literally called him "Master." In the Greek language that referral of "Rabbi" means "Master. Therefore, Nicodemus referred to Jesus as a master teacher who came from God.

Nicodemus recognized something that most people overlook concerning Jesus…He was an exceptional teacher throughout His earthly ministry. Jesus was informed on history and had above average knowledge of the Torah, the Psalms, and prophetic books. Jesus quoted from them and could articulate and facilitate a thorough discussion on various topics. In addition, Jesus could intelligently discuss politics, laws and legislation, cultural customs, and societal etiquette. Jesus was filled with Biblical knowledge and natural knowledge as well as the Spirit of God.

Evangelists must follow the model of Jesus and possess both Biblical and natural knowledge as well as be filled with the Spirit of God to be a master teacher. The problem with people today is that they are lazy and do not have the passion, ambition, nor the disciplined focus it takes to be a master teacher like Jesus. Master teachers must read, study, and collect information from diverse pools which eventually molds them into a master teacher. Master teachers are not one dimensional but rather they have a plethora of information to pull from.

Tenured evangelists have read, studied, and learned from a multiplicity of sources and cultures. They have engaged in and connected with people and served on projects which exposed them to high level information. Seasoned evangelists sat at tables with career professional, entrepreneurs, and ministry leaders long before becoming an evangelist.

In addition, evangelists have interacted with every generation from toddlers thru the retired community and inhaled information from every source, resource, conversation, and interaction. This is one reason why evangelists are great teachers because their information is vast and massive and not restricted to their religious beliefs, ethnic community, generation era, political affiliation, nor their current culture and climate. This process prepares evangelists to be master teachers. Their intellectual depth and cognitive range are not preference, feelings based. Conversely, teaching evangelist's positions are steep internal treasures of information they have investigated, collected, and stored in an internal vault over their entire lifespan.

Other ministry gifts do well when their career is closely aligned with their ministry gift i.e apostles build so they are good in careers which allows them to build. Pastors are shepherds so their career will flourish when they are allowed to care for people as a vocation.

However, evangelists are versatile and will have several career paths, business adventures, and ministry assignments throughout their life. They will often begin as consumers where they are exposed to information and digest the information. When that level has been exhausted, evangelists will become bored and aspire for something different and a greater challenge. Eventually, they will progress to become the teacher in careers and ministries where they were once the student.

Because of the evangelist's versatility, they can enter multiple career fields throughout their life and excel. However, to maximize evangelists' full potential, they must be placed in environments where they have diversity; not the same job, the same way, same people, same, same, same…nope. Evangelists need to be where they can interact with diverse people doing a multiplicity of things.

Furthermore, if you really desire to tap into the core of evangelists so they can produce maximum fruit, give them short-term, important assignments. Most evangelists are fulfilled by purposed-based assignments and not by money, prestige, nor exposure. Evangelists want to make meaningful contributions but make it short-term so they do not become bored and uninterested.

Hear this clearly…most evangelists are not graced for long term assignments; not even long-term teaching assignments with top-financial pay and exposure. Because of the itinerant nature of the evangelist, long-term assignments are dangerous in the hands of evangelists because soon they will desire to move around and will start seeking the next thing connected to their purpose.

Because of the need for an evangelist to be diverse, they are *"temporarily"* graced by God to multitask and will do a great job, for a short period of time, then the itch for "different/new" will need to be scratched. Teaching is a great way to scratch the itch for evangelists because teaching have limitless (new) topics where they can feel useful and be effective, which will hold off boredom. Lastly, teaching is part of the 5-ministry graces which Jesus gave to the church to equip the church; evangelists who teach can help with that assignment too.

Therefore, evangelists who teach is essential in Christian churches because they get the evangelist, and a teacher encapsulated into one. In addition, because evangelists are diverse, they enjoy independent study and will perform the necessary research for an in-depth, highly intellectual presentation.

Remember, evangelists who teach have a wealth of information on various topics where people can benefit. Evangelists are *not* teachers in the five-fold ministry gifts because teaching is not their primary gift. However, they can teach as the Holy Spirit anoints them to complete tasks.

Teacher Antithesis: Pride. When a teacher becomes overly confident in themselves and in their knowledge, they are in danger of being under the toxicity of pride. This is a common occurrence of teachers who have longevity in an area or a subject matter. They take ownership of the space and become rigid and inflexible to new ideas and even new information. This prideful behavior is detrimental and will cause stagnation in the teacher and pause creativity in the organization.

I Corinthians 8:1 says,

"...Knowledge puffeth up."

The above Scripture does not mean we should be ignorant and illiterate. Neither does it mean we should not pursue knowledge or seek new information. That is not how that passage should be interpreted but rather it can be accurately interpreted as...

*"Dependence on personal knowledge alone
can cause one to become prideful."*
(LDJ, 2024)

This is something evangelists must guard themselves against. Because they possess Biblical knowledge in addition to other information, it is easier for them to become entangled in empty sometimes hostile debates. Evangelists herald the true message of salvation through Jesus Christ, and they are often resisted, tested, and confronted with erroneous doctrine and half-truths. However, one must discern if they are in a teachable moment or on a road of an endless unfruitful discussion which often leads to emotional disagreements and antagonistic arguments.

If evangelists become emotionally engaged, their discernment will be compromised, and pride can easily enter and influence the evangelist to win the argument by any means available to them. Their knowledge will then become a weapon used to kill and destroy others. Evangelists cannot allow their pride in the knowledge they possess on a topic to lead them into a contested, heated debate for the mere satisfaction of winning an argument. We must be bigger and better than that as evangelists.

Kill pride and teach people when the listeners are ready and prepared to receive. If the heart of the listener is not open to hear and learn, then simply become silent. They may be ready in the future, but you do not want to blow the opportunity to empower them later by embarrassing them publicly with your knowledge. Evangelist are teachers!

~ PREACHER ~

Evangelists are **PREACHERS**! However, most of their preaching is not done on a Sunday morning nor behind a wood/glass podium with a microphone in their hand. Absolutely not! Quite frankly some evangelists dread preaching on a Sunday morning with a microphone. They are more comfortable with a small group of people and without a microphone. There is nothing wrong about that. In fact, we need more evangelists who are not chasing the microphone but are willing to preach in smaller settings.

The main concern is does the evangelist preach, not where or how they preach. Every evangelist should preach but be aware that how they preach is connected to their innate personalities. Most introverted evangelists may prefer smaller groups or speak individually with people like at a coffee shop, or on the phone or even through text messages. On the other hand, extroverted evangelists may be more comfortable with crowds, churches and conferences, and any other public venue.

Conversely, do not assume every woman who preach is an evangelist! Most women who preach are just preachers and not evangelists. Today, we see women who have the title of evangelist on their promotional flyers and are contracted to preach at conferences because they presented themselves as an evangelist, but they are not evangelists. To investigate this claim simply ask them (1) how many people have they led to Jesus and (2) how many people have they discipled?

Most of them, if honest will admit that they do not evangelize nor make personal investments into people's Christian development; they just love to preach which means they are itinerant preachers and not evangelists.

Placing the title of evangelist on women who preach has been a long practice of religious misogyny in Christian churches. Because male presbytery refused to accept women as their equal in ministry, they gave them the title of evangelist to demean them and make them smaller. This was done to exert control and authority over women and to keep them in an insignificant place in ministry. Unfortunately, the shrinkage of female ministers was executed under the title of evangelist.

In recent church history and within certain denominations, women were not received as preachers or pastors, and nor were they able to occupy any other significant position of influence because those titles and roles were reserved for men only. However, women were received as evangelists because they intended for it to be an inferior position reserved for the male's discretion and not as a Biblical, gender-neutral function.

This is one reason evangelists did not receive official ministry training nor equipping, affirmations nor validation. However, they were permitted to teach small classes like Sunday school, lead women's groups, taught children's ministry, and book clubs. Under a progressive pastor, women were able to speak (not preach) on Women's Day, but not in the actual pulpit. Some church's cultural view was that women were spiritually inferior to men and the title of evangelist was used as a weapon to propagate that perspective. Therefore, women refused to be identified as evangelists because it did not "agree" with their spirit.

Women who were called evangelists were not expected to grow, be developed in their calling, nor lead others. Being an evangelist was just a placeholder, pseudo title, but not an authentic function in most churches. Being an evangelist was not about acceptance into the five-fold ministry as one of God's called and chosen servants, but rather an evangelist title was a mere distinction between men and women ministers in some Christian cultures.

This is the demonic oppressive, rejected spirit which hovers around evangelists today! If evangelists were honest, they would admit that they feel oppressed, overlooked, rejected, insignificant and under-appreciated. This spirit was ushered into evangelism by foul misogynistic people who devalued and misused the office of the evangelist to cover their own insecurities. For this cause, it is difficult to get authentic evangelists to confidently be and function as evangelists. They will flood into other ministries because it feels better and its less demonic warfare.

Lastly, preaching is one of the primary responsibilities of an evangelist. Again, that does not mean they must preach inside of the church, behind the pulpit with a microphone...not at all! However, evangelists should preach the Gospel (virgin birth, death, burial, resurrection, and ascension) of Jesus Christ. Where they choose to preach and how they deliver the message is at their discretion.

Be informed that when evangelists preach, their messages will be different than pastors, prophets, and apostles. To the trained skilled ear, you will hear the pastor's heart, pioneering apostolic language, and even prophetic utterances when an evangelist preaches. However, the primary theme of evangelistic messages is Jesus's salvation and deliverance.

Evangelist's messages are informative and highly persuasive. They preach to persuade people to make a decision for Jesus; either to accept Him for the 1st time (new believers), or to continue to trust Him (current believers). Evangelist's sermon will consist of several critical ingredients: Bible stories, personal stories, statistics, and a call to action.

- **Bible Stories:** Evangelists will often begin with a story or parable from the Bible as their centered-focal point of the message. Evangelists are deeply connected to and dependent upon the Bible for information and they use the Bible's information to persuade others of Jesus's sin sacrifice available to everyone.

- **Personal Stories:** Evangelists will use personal stories to enhance a point in their message or to demonstrate their own relevance and connection to a topic. This is to highlight Jesus's power and ability to rescue others from similar situations. Personal stories should never highlight the evangelist as the hero but rather always highlight Jesus as the focal point and inspire others to trust Him. After her encounter and experience with Jesus, the woman at the well (John 4:29, KJV) told the people in Samaria "Come, see a man which told me all things that ever I did: is not this the Christ?" Evangelists will use their personal encounter and experiences with Jesus to inspire and persuade others. It's commonly referred to as a testimony.

I've been watching a mega-pastor in Houston, Texas for many years. One thing is certain with this pastor, whom many say is an evangelist, he always mentions how his church acquired their church facility, which was formerly the home an NBA basketball team. When the church tried to buy the stadium initially, they were declined. After several attempts and many miracles, the church bought the stadium, and they currently hold their church services there.

Although they have been in the church for over a decade, the pastor often includes the testimony of how they purchased the stadium into his message; many of his messages. You would think that after all these years, with the same church members and a regular television audience that the pastor would stop sharing that *same* story, get another testimony, or get an updated version of the story. Nope! It's the evangelist's discretion when to share, how often they share, and what parts of the story they share with which audience.

When I share my personal testimony of deliverance, I always tailor it for the audience I am currently speaking because every audience is not the same. There are parts of my story which helps a certain demographic of people and other parts of my story which benefits another demographic of people. However, sharing a personal story can be beneficial only if the proper story is shared with the proper audience at the proper time. Do not share a story with one audience because it went well when you shared it with another audience. Measure and assess the audience. The goal is to always persuade and inspire people to trust Jesus and that can happen through a personal story.

- **Statistics:** Statistics is data used to support positional statements. Statistics gives credibility when the original source is properly and accurately cited. Statistics can be beneficial to an evangelist's message and cause listeners to *"lean-in"* to what is being said.

  However, most people do not like to use statistics in their messages because it takes work to locate stats which are specifically applicable to the message. You must read books, research articles, and verify posts/tweets to find a statistic that will help the message. It is also good to use stats and/or statements which are opposed to your position. It gives the listener another perspective and you can discuss why you oppose the opinion which opposed you.

Using statistics is a good habit to massage into your research method. It will expand and increase your knowledge base and keep you relevant on what's being discussed in culture. In addition, it breaks off laziness and keeps you humble by knowing that others have a perspective too which should be considered.

- **Call to Action:** As an evangelist, the "Call-to-Action" is usually the invitation to Jesus aka altar call. Every evangelist must invite people to Jesus!

Call-to-Action is a common component of public speaking. It is usually at the end of the speech but is the most important part of the speech. It is the real reason why you are speaking.

Call-to-Action is where listeners are encouraged to act and/or make a decision. It is an important and critical part of the presentation and must executed with skill, excellence, and compassionate sensitivity. When politicians speak, they usually end with a Call-to-Action to (1) Register and vote for them or (2) Donate money to their campaign. Politicians travel thousands of miles to speak to an audience for a few minutes only to call people into action by asking for their vote or to donate money.

Politicians understand how important the Call-to-Action is to their agenda. Because of it, they share their message with as many as people as possible.

Politicians believes that the more people who hear them, increases the chance that people will connect with them, and the more people who connects with them, the more people who will respond positively to their message. As a result, after politicians have delivered their message, and while they still have the attention of people, they ask the people to respond; they call them into action!

Just like politicians believe in their message and courageously make an appeal for people to respond, every evangelist should do the same: speak, then Call-to-Action. If evangelists do this habitually, the Gospel will contagiously spread and become a powerful, irresistible vortex where people will be ferociously drawn into, and lives will be transformed. Oftentimes people do not respond to the Gospel because we did not give a Call-to-Action.

When evangelists preach, routinely their Call-to-Action resembles an appeal to either accept Jesus (new believer) or to strengthen faith in Jesus (current believer). Keep in mind that a call-to-action led by an evangelist may also include prayer for healing, deliverance ministry, and prophetic words (encouragement). Evangelists can never overlook nor under-estimate the power of the Call-to-Action.

As a young evangelist, I felt bad about my message if I made an altar appeal for salvation as my Call-to-Action and no one came forward. I felt like I did not preach or teach good enough. The silence in the room was loud while I waited for someone to respond to the Call-to-Action, and often it destabilized my emotions. I struggled internally and secretly wondered if I was a true evangelist because people did not respond.

In moments like that, it can be several reasons why people don't respond or come forward. In short, some people deal with shame and embarrassment and do not want to walk down an aisle for everyone to see them; other people want to think about it and decide later. With all the schemes and improprieties in churches lately, people are more hesitant to respond openly in church based on emotional stimulation.

As an evangelist, understand that if people respond to your Call-to-Action or if they do not respond by coming forward, all of it is up to God and the people; you have no control of that. Be content in the fact that you delivered the message, and you gave an opportunity for people to respond and receive of Jesus.

Preacher Antithesis: Avoid preaching prostitution! Which is preaching for personal profit. Preachers have tainted God's idea of a preacher by making the message about them and bending it for personal profit. This is the signet of a motivational preacher; they preach so that it sounds good to the ear, but the motive is to be good for their pocket and their platform.

One way to avoid preaching prostitution is to frequently preach in smaller arenas or give impromptu messages in places where no one will know what you are doing. In this era of social media with limitless cameras, preach in places where you will not be recorded. Preach in coffee shops, hospitals, nursing homes, prisons, gas stations, laundry mats, banks, Walmart, on the job, sport arenas/games, and etc.

When preaching becomes more about you, the money, and popularity (likes, comments, shares and followers), rather than about Jesus and changing lives, then you have become a prostitute who is being pimped by preaching. Unfortunately, that is part of the problem in Christian churches. Preaching prostitutes should not be preaching the glorious Gospel of Jesus Christ.

A preacher's assignment is to advance the Kingdom of God with the message of salvation and deliverance. Preaching is to strengthen and empower believers so they can then go and bring in others into the Kingdom of God. Although there is an art and skill to preaching, exegetical and hermeneutical, the message should always point people to Jesus and He should be the center of the message. Lastly, preaching should always be presented so people can make a decision to become a follower of Jesus, or preaching should cause faith to deepen in Jesus.

However, evangelists are preachers, and they preach the Gospel with emphasis on Jesus the Savior who heals and delivers. Evangelists set up opportunities for Jesus to liberate captives and perform miracles. Evangelist's sermons are often extracted from the Gospels and are often connected to a miracle or a parable, infused with personal stories and spiritual demonstrations through prophesy, healing, and/or deliverance.

Evangelists are a different kind of a preacher, distinguished from pastoral, prophetic, and apostolic preachers. I did not say they were better than other preachers, I said they were different! When under the anointing of an evangelist who preaches, you will be encouraged to live life through Jesus Christ and under the power of the Holy Spirit. Evangelists are preachers!

~ DELIVERANCE ~

Evangelists operate in **DELIVERANCE**! They cast out demons. Casting out demons is Biblical; it was part of Jesus ministry, the apostle's ministry, Philip's ministry and should be part of every evangelist's ministry.

Surely evangelists don't cast out demons daily, weekly or in some cases not even monthly. However, evangelists should be comfortable to cast out demons when needed by the authority in name of Jesus and through the power in the blood of Jesus.

For a certainty, evangelists will be confronted by demonic interference as they share the message of salvation because satan hates that message which frees people from his control. Satan wants people to remain bound so he will "show-out" aka "manifest" to distract or intimidate the evangelist which is a fear tactic to stop or silence the message. As a result, when demons manifest, evangelists must be ready to unapologetically and without hesitation cast them out!

However, evangelists must improve on how they cast out demons. In church culture, people yell, scream, throw water/oil, wrestle, and perform all sorts of theatrics as they cast out demons. It's all a religious show much like the show on Mt. Caramel with Elijah vs. the prophets of Baal as recorded in 1 Kings 18:26-29 (KJV).

"And they took the bullock which was given them, and they dressed it, and called on the name of Baal from morning even until noon, saying O Baal, hear us. But there was no voice, nor any that answered. And they leaped upon the altar which was made. (27) And it came to pass at noon, that Elijah mocked them, and said, Cry aloud:: for he is a god; either he is talking, or he is pursuing, or he is in a journey, or peradventure he sleepeth, and must be awaked. (28) And they cried aloud, and cut themselves after their manner with knives and lancets, till the blood gushed out upon them. (29) And it came to pass, when midday was past, and they prophesied until the time of offering of the evening sacrifice, that there was neither voice nor any to answer, not any that regarded."

That is what religious shenanigans look like! It has the appearance that something deeply spiritual is happening because of the activity but factually nothing is happening in the spirit realm. It's all circus smoke and mirrors to create an illusion, just religious foolishness.

The prophets of Baal went to great lengths to prove that their god had power. They started at midday and continued until the evening trying to make something happen. They leaped and jumped on the altar but nothing significant happened. They cut themselves with knives until they bled but nothing spiritual happened. They screamed until they were hoarse and still nothing! Nothing happened. Nothing happened because their god did not have power. It was just a religious show for the amusement of people, but absolutely nothing substantial occurred in the spiritual realm.

Years ago, this passage convicted me. It made me question why was I hoarse and exhausted when I cast out demons? It took me 2-3 days to recover from a deliverance service. I inquired, "What was the physical drain on my body and why was it that way?" Could it be that I attempted to do in my own natural strength what only God was able to accomplish spiritually?

Don't get me wrong, I still believe in deliverance. I believe we must cast out the devil using Jesus' name and apply His blood because that's where the power lies...its in Jesus! I believe this. However, most of what is done in Christian deliverance services is NOT God, Jesus the Christ, nor His angels...it's religious shenanigans for the entertainment and amusement of naïve, unlearned people to stimulate their emotions. Nothing more. And for this cause, we have the same results as the prophets of Baal had...*nothing*!

God did not move with Baal's prophets, just as He's not moving among most of the deliverance ministers today regardless of how loud they talk, yell, and spit. Regardless of the number of social media followers, big towels, catholic priest apparel, cross on the chest, staff in hand, supersized entourage, squinted eyes, and a deep slow talking voice does not equal God's anointing, nor does it confirm that an individual is working with the Spirit of God. It is not God if the results cannot be proven, measured, verified, and brings Him glory.

As I studied Jesus and how He conducted deliverance, it revolutionized how I administered deliverance. Jesus rebuked and commanded demons to come out. Jesus did not yell, scream, wrestle, pin people to the floor, nor shake them into reality…He used His words, "Come Out," and exercised His authority over them, and the demons obeyed.

Deliverance Antithesis: Evangelists will encounter demonic activity probably more frequently than other ministry gifts because they are extracting people from satan's grip and liberating them from his control; and he won't be happy!

Therefore, the devil will do anything to ensure he does not lose people by way of evangelists. As a result, satan will increase his attack on evangelists to intimidate and traumatize them into silence. Oddly, this does not begin when the evangelist enter ministry, but rather satan's attack on evangelists can start as early as in the womb or during early childhood.

Most evangelists have experienced hell i.e. molestation, rape, abandonment, rejection, loss of parents, loss of children, addictions (sex, alcohol and drugs, gambling, food) imprisonment, emotional instability, betrayals, etc. by their teenage years. Because of this, they need massive deliverance just to be sane and make it through their own chaotic life. The relentless invitations from hell to commit suicide or to revert back to old behaviors is the constant battle of evangelists which requires 100% dependency on the Holy Spirit. This is why evangelists are great people to administer deliverance...they are regular benefactors of deliverance!

Therefore, evangelists are assured of their power over satan given to them by Jesus Christ. They became assured as they watched Jesus deliver them daily. This is why they are confident in Jesus's delivering power. If an evangelist is not convinced that Jesus's power will move through them, they will definitely be bullied into doubt, insecurity, and fear by satan. Mark 16:17 (NKJV), Jesus says,

> *"And these signs will follow them who believe;*
> *In My name, they will cast out demons..."*

The prerequisite to casting out demons is that you must believe! Satan is just like the school-yard-bully who only terrorizes people who are afraid. If the devil smells fear in you, he will capitalize on that fear and make you choke on it. Subsequently, your confidence must be in (1) The name of Jesus (2) The blood of Jesus and (3) Your personal deliverance experience; these will cover and protect you!

Therefore, evangelists must not be afraid to cast out demons but rather confidently do it in Jesus Name, under the power of His blood.

Another issue to be on alert in deliverance ministry is that evangelists can go to extremes and see demons everywhere, in everything, and in everyone. They become '*spooky*' and difficult to tolerate in everyday life. Being spooky will hinder the ability to relate to people and you will seem odd.

Evangelist must know the devil is not in everything nor is he responsible for everything. Satan is not God, and we must not make him equal to God. Satan is not omnipotent (all powerful), omnipresent (everywhere at the same time), nor omniscient (all knowing), only God. Therefore, he is not involved in every matter which occurs in the world. Some of life's unpleasantries are caused by personal choice and lack of preparation. A more adequate perspective is that some things are consequences and not demonic interference. Know the difference before you start slinging oil and rolling up your sleeves to fight.

Chapter Three
~ Genre of Evangelists ~

I was astonished when I discovered there were various types of evangelists, an entire genre. My frame of reference of an evangelist was clouded by the evangelists which I saw as a child in my baptist church. I thought an evangelist was wild, undisciplined, and an unrestrained preacher who only preached the evening service on the 5th Sunday of the month. Usually, evangelists were from out-of-state and was unknown to the people and city where they preached. They were classified as radical because they walked on top of chairs, slung oil, and carried supersized handkerchiefs. Those evangelists were unlike most reserved senior pastors in our denomination. They were more of a hermeneutic circus show for entertainment and amusement.

Because of my view of an evangelist, I was perplexed when I was labeled an evangelist because most of what I saw in evangelists was unlike my personality. It was after I studied Jesus and other evangelists that I realized I had a misinterpretation of evangelists. This happened because I never had an authentic evangelistic model to shape my perspective of an evangelist. Sadly, back then most churches could not even define evangelists, let alone provide an evangelistic model for anyone to follow.

Shortly after I started preaching, I saw Billy Graham preach on television and it changed my life! He preached one of the parables of Jesus and thousands of people responded to his invitation to accept Jesus as their

Savior. I was fascinated! I was not aware that he was an evangelist at the time. I simply admired the way he preached.

As a result, I hunted Billy Graham down like a lion in search of their stolen cubs! I watched Billy Graham's old television programs; I bought his books and purchased his DVD's. I thought, "I want to preach like this man!" I noticed that Billy Graham regularly preached from the Gospels. Consequently, I read the gospels over and over and over again so I could inherit the grace to preach the Gospel like him. I prayed and asked God to give me whatever anointed grace Billy Graham possessed to preach the Gospel. I craved supernatural revelation and a distinct delivery of the gospels.

In recent years I wondered how Evangelist Billy Graham would be defined today. Don't get me wrong, I understand he was an evangelist, but what type of an evangelist? Listen carefully, Billy Graham was not an average evangelist who preached messages and hosted community outreaches. He was unique, different, and far above other evangelists. Billy Graham did his job in a manner which very few people can replicate. He traveled the world, filled stadiums and arenas, and he had an audience with nearly every president of the United States during his ministry span.

As I grew spiritually and learned more about the apostolic grace, it was then the revelation of an apostolic evangelist appeared through my study. That was new revelation and seemed quite odd to connect the term apostolic to the evangelist. "Hmmm, an apostolic evangelist? What is an apostolic evangelist?" I thought.

~ THE APOSTOLIC EVANGELIST ~

The title "Apostolic Evangelist" may be a new term to some; however, the characteristics of apostolic evangelists are more common than you may realize.

The term "Apostolic" is a Biblical term which points to Jesus and His apostles in the book of Acts. It leans to the origin of the church as we have come to know it. The term apostolic can be defined as, "One who charters new terrain, whose success cannot be *easily* duplicated, a pioneer, a trailblazer." In short, apostolic means one who can create...because of the connection to the creative God, the ability to create is within apostolic people and they have discovered ways to manifest it in their life and ministry.

The definition of the word "apostolic" would disqualify most of today's ministers who call themselves apostles. They have not created nor pioneered anything and most of what they have done is old and archaic passageways which can be *easily* duplicated by almost anyone!

The apostolic crop today lacks the ability to pioneer a new distinctive work. They are underdeveloped, under-processed, and over-served in exposure. They start churches and networks but most are imitations of the person they admire or the network they are connected; nothing new nor unique.

On the other hand, the uniqueness of the word "Apostolic" is that it can be used as both a noun and a verb. Therefore, a person can be apostolic, and a movement can be apostolic as well. What is most intriguing, both can operate simultaneously within one person. Yes, a person can be apostolic, and their ministry can be apostolic which makes it miraculous in its foundation. This affirms that miracles should be the signet throughout an apostolic ministry. There should never be a deficit in miraculous testimonies in an apostolic ministry.

In retrospect, when the life and ministries of Evangelist Billy Graham or Aimee Semple McPherson and others are examined, it is apparent how they qualify as apostolic evangelists. They created miraculous ministries which has not been duplicated, not even decades and centuries later.

Evangelist Billy Graham possessed an anointing to invite people to accept Jesus and thousands responded. Evangelist Aimee Semple McPherson possessed a healing anointing so unique where California residents discharged family members from hospitals and brought them to her church services to be healed…and they were healed! With Billy Graham and Aimee Semple-McPherson, their ministry proved they were apostolic evangelists by the true definition of the term. They pioneered and chartered new terrain which cannot be easily replicated.

However, don't be discouraged. To become an apostolic evangelist, it will take time; time to build and time for what was built to yield results. Although it has been said that apostles are born, it takes time for the seal or the evidence of an apostle's work to visibly manifest and confirm their apostolic assignment. The same is true of apostolic evangelists, time will reveal those who are apostolic evangelists. However, the path of an apostolic evangelist is more common and clearer today than in the past.

Most apostolic evangelists spend a considerable amount of time as evangelists preaching the Gospel, making disciples, conducting outreaches and training believers. After a while, some evangelists move into the function of a pastor. The evangelist will have sheep/people which reports directly to them whom they care for and are responsible to nurture, teach, and develop. The pastor's role gives evangelists the structure required to lead people, and it gives them needed experience on the administrative side of ministry. Most evangelists love people but secretly despise the administrative side of ministry. In fact, I have renamed administration ministry as the "Red-Tape" ministry because it's too technical for me although it is necessary.

The pastor's role creates a solid ring of fire around evangelists to usher them into apostolic function. This is congruent in the maturation process of evangelists who will later become apostolic evangelists. If evangelists apply lessons learned and knowledge gained as both an evangelist and as a pastor, not only they will manage people well, but they will also govern situations with a steady and stable hand which is an advantage as an apostolic evangelist.

Let me be clear about this, it's not required to add "apostolic" to your title or get a business card with "apostolic evangelist" in your name. The fruit of what was created, built, and how it has been sustained will be the needed proof and the seal that you are indeed an apostolic evangelist.

Examine yourself; Are you doing what everyone else is doing? Can anyone who desires replicate what you have built? If the answer is yes, it may be premature to secure the title of apostolic evangelist. An apostolic evangelist does things which others cannot do nor even thought to attempt. Remember, you must create and pioneer something new, and be a model for others to follow, as that is the seal of a true apostolic evangelist.

~ THE PROPHETIC EVANGELIST ~

The prophetic evangelist is a more common type of evangelist today. This is partly because of insecure evangelists who need to add the word prophetic to their ministry to increase attendance and gain popularity. This is dangerous and this person is usually a ministry novice, seeking attention and a platform more than they are seeking to lead people to Jesus.

However, the prophetic evangelist is an authentic function. It is an evangelist who is graced prophetically and regularly use prophetic utterances in their evangelistic ministry. Nevertheless, they are an authentic evangelist as their primary ministry gift, and they don't manipulate the prophetic for personal gain, profit, or influence.

Keep in mind that every evangelist will have a measure of prophetic grace. It is a must! Evangelists must have the ability to hear from God in real-time and receive His instructions/information for themselves and for the people they are evangelizing.

With Jesus being our evangelistic model, He spoke of His ability to hear what the Father said. Furthermore, Jesus confirmed that He spoke what the Father told Him to say, John 12:50 (KJV).

"...whatsoever I speak therefore,
even as the Father said unto me, so I speak."

This gives evangelists permission to operate prophetically. We can confidently say what God give us to say, whether it is a preached word or a prophetic word. However, the key is to ensure you heard from God and that you are saying what God has said, and not what you feel nor what you want to say to a person.

Do not attach God's name to your personal opinion nor your preference. That is manipulation and witchcraft to use the prophetic to stimulate someone's soulish emotions for personal benefit. Therefore, before you say, "God said" be sure that God actually said it.

The best way to ensure prophetic accuracy is to connect your words to His Word; the Bible. When prophetic words are heavily doused with Scriptures, scriptural references, and Biblical principles, it is more likely to be an accurate prophetic word. When rooted in Scriptures, it won't matter to you if the person "receive it" or not. If they reject the prophetic word which was saturated in the Word, you won't feel rejected nor take it personal. You will better understand they rejected the "Word of God" and not you.

I Corinthians 14:3 says that we are to prophesy to edify, encourage, and comfort which means everyone has the ability to prophesy. As evangelists, this can be complexed as a portion of our ministry is to allow the Holy Spirit to convict of sin and often that does not feel like encouragement, edification and neither is it comforting. However, evangelists should still find ways to prophesy (encourage, edify and comfort) in their messages and interactions. Usually, the inspiring part of the message is when it is revealed that Jesus can save, heal, and deliver from it all.

Furthermore, 1 Corinthians 14:24-25 says that if someone is a non-believer, when that person is prophesied to, they become convinced and judged, as secrets in their heart are revealed. This will cause them to worship God and tell people that God truly moves in that place and in the person who prophesied to them.

Evangelists should use the prophetic in their evangelistic ministry as it can persuade people of God's existence and His love for them, as well as validate the ministry of the evangelist. However, evangelists should never manipulate or deceive people through the prophetic to draw people to themselves.

Never forget that the testimony of Jesus Christ is the Spirit of prophesy (Revelation 19:10b, KJV). People should be drawn to Jesus and reminded of Jesus, and not an individual when true prophetic ministry is administered.

~ THE REVIVALIST EVANGELIST ~

Man-oh-man do we need revival! Revival is defined by Webster's dictionary as, "An evangelistic meeting intended to *reawaken* interest in religion."

Don't be fooled by fancy fliers and predetermined, propagandized programs. Revivals are orchestrated by our sovereign God! No minister or pastor can spontaneously mandate, preschedule, or manufacture an authentic Holy Spirit led revival. Simply because a local church hosted several meetings within a short span of time does not accurately attest that those meetings were a revival.

The first Biblical revival modeled what revivals are composed of, and subsequent revivals were shaped and formed in the image and likeness of the original revival in Acts chapter 2. Let's review Acts chapter 2 as our template for revival.

- Acts 2:1-4: On the day of Pentecost, one-hundred and twenty people were filled with the Holy Spirit.
- Acts 2:5-12: Various ethnicities witnessed the miracle of the Holy Spirit in conjunction with Apostle Peter and the others. They heard them speak in their own, natural language although though they had no previous training in foreign languages.
- Acts 2:13: They were mocked, and accused of drinking *new* wine (how prophetic?)
- Acts 2:14: Peter boldly preached an uncompromised, straight forward, in-your-face Gospel.
- Acts 2:41: The people who heard Peter, received his message and about three thousand souls were added.

~ SIGNS OF REVIVAL ~

- Revivals are orchestrated by our sovereign God. The Holy Spiri will be at the wheel initiating and directing traffic! Not a man or woman. You don't need a human headliner for a Holy Spirit led revival.

- A colossal number of people will hear and be impacted, not just your family or your local church family. The revival may start small, but the wind of the Holy Spirit will blow it up and hundreds of thousands will be impacted.
- A true revival will be mocked, and false accusations and false labels will occur. People will laugh at it, try to discredit the people connected to it, ostracize it and overall try to disprove its authenticity.
- Powerful, direct preaching of the uncompromised gospel will cause an awakening in listeners and a flood of new converts will be the result. God will be worshipped, and Jesus will be exalted, not a preacher, church, denomination, or a network.
- Innumerable decisions are made for Jesus during the entire span of a revival to accept Him for the first time. In addition, backsliders return to Jesus and the overwhelmed will receive restored strength to continue their journey.
- Miracles of healing are evident during a revival. Physical healings and emotional healings, in addition to families being healed and unity restored.

Our churches and cities need revival! We need to be *reawakened* to the power of the Holy Spirit, which was lured to sleep by religious, divisive, non-Biblical views. However, the precursor to a *reawakening* in the earth today, is an *awakening* in those who carry the gospel message of salvation and deliverance...*The Evangelist*! When evangelists wake up, then the Gospel will once again be shared as a priority, and we will see a *reawakening* and ultimately revival.

In all truth, the world is at its capacity with lethargic, passionless, scared to be persecuted, so-called evangelists who only want to preach and prophesy within the four walls of a church because they are trying to be famous rather than end a spiritual famine. As long as evangelists are asleep or chasing personal prosperity and fame, we will continue to scream, "Lord send revival!"

Consequently, before revival comes, there must be vessels which can usher in revival. That is not to say that other ministry gifts cannot be canals of revival. However, it unquestionably means that evangelists should spark revival in their sphere of influence. There should be an uptick in people's interest in Jesus and they should become quite inquisitive concerning Him when a fire-ball evangelist is in their presence.

Unlike other prototypes of the evangelist, there are effective models of the revivalist evangelist such as: Maria Woodworth-Etter, William J. Seymour, Dwight L. Moody, Billy Sunday, Charles Spurgeon, and Kathryn Kuhlman. The aforementioned names were revivalist's evangelists, but their administration and demonstration of their gifts varied from person-to-person.

With our predecessors and examples of revivalist evangelists, evangelists everywhere should be inspired because God will use the gifts, He anointed *you* with from birth. There's no need to be a clone, replica, or take on another person's evangelistic preaching style because God wants to use you as He created and gifted you. Neither should you attempt to erect an unassigned healing ministry because God will use whatever gift you possess to spark revival if you will allow the Holy Spirit to lead you.

"But we have this treasure in earthen vessels,
that the excellency of the power
may be of God, and not of us."

The above verse from 2 Corinthians 4:7 (KJV), must be in the near-view of revivalist evangelists as they will experience God's anointing to supernaturally gather people and even perform miracles of healing, in ways that most preachers will never experience. If the revivalists are not careful, the devil will seduce them to believe that it is their wisdom, their marketing strategy, or network connections which has brought about miracles and ministry success. Revivalists must be fully persuaded and totally dependent upon the sovereignty of God and the power of the Holy Spirit to understand that it is all because of God and for His glory alone!

Sadly, many revivalists in the 20th century stumbled publicly and lost their influence and platform because they lost sight of God. Their focus shifted to make more money, build houses, and to expand their personal platforms for their benefit. As a result, God's grace lifted, and they were exposed for sexual improprieties and financial embezzlements. It was sad to watch anointed, knowledgeable, influential revivalists who led millions to Jesus, fall from grace. However, it should be a reminder to everyone that we are not above God's judgment. God will always protect His name even if He must ruin yours.

Therefore, if you have a healing grace, God will use your gift of healing to usher in revival. If you are a gifted preacher, God will use your preaching gift to bring revival. If you move in verifiable miracles, God will use your miracle ministry as a catalyst for revival.

As a revivalist evangelist, the most important thing to remember is allow the Holy Spirit to work revival through you; and yes, you are obligated to direct all of the glory to God. Again, remember that…

"For we have this treasure in earthen vessels,
that the excellency of the power
may be of God, and not of us."
2 Corinthians 4:7 (KJV)

~ 21ST CENTURY EVANGELIST ~

I read a Scripture that brought me under immense pressure. I felt pressure because I felt Jesus expected me to do greater than Him. Logically, I fully understood Jesus would never request something of me which would be impossible for me to accomplish. Therefore, I pondered how could anyone fulfill John 14:12.

"Verily, verily, I say unto you,
He that believeth on me, the works that I do
shall he do also; and greater works than these
shall he do; because I go unto my Father."
John 14:12 (KJV)

There are many Scriptures in the Bible which can be intimidating like "More than a conqueror," "Chase a thousand," "Head and not the tail, lender and not the borrower,' etc. However, few Scriptures are more intimidating than John 14:12 (KJV) when Jesus says, (1)

We are to replicate His works and (2) We are to exceed His works!

What? Jesus wants believers to do greater works than He did during His earthly ministry? The answer is an emphatic, "Yes!" Surely that is intimidating when you consider the vast body of ministry work Jesus accomplished in under four years i.e. He fed thousands, restored natural sight to the blind, unplugged deaf ears, restored life to the deceased, transformed water into wine, walked on water, rebuked storms, effortlessly casted out demons, and healed sick bodies. Not many people believe they can do exactly what Jesus did, and probably no one believes they can do *greater* than Jesus.

The key word in John 14:12 (KJV) is the word "Greater." The root word in greater is the word great which means "remarkable and out of the ordinary!" Therefore, when Jesus says, "Greater works shall you do" it implies that Jesus expects believers to be more remarkable, more effective, and more productive than Him. Under that interpretation it does seem like Jesus gave us a humanly impossible task to fulfill. For assurance, few are confident that they can be more remarkable than Jesus.

However, upon further investigation of the Scriptures, we see that Jesus gave us the prescription to how we are to accomplish the "greater" works depicted in John 14:12 (KJV). Take a look at John 14:13 (KJV).

"And whatsoever ye shall ask in my name, that will I do, that the Father may be glorified in the Son."

When that Scripture is closely examined, one can conclude for anyone to do *greater* works than Jesus, Jesus

Himself must do it! The Scripture clearly says that if we request Jesus's assistance in our quest for greater works, Jesus Himself will actually do the work through us. That is amazing!

This revelation frees us from attempting to manufacture results through our own strength which we will never measure up to Jesus' success. However, if we invoke Jesus into all of our endeavors, He will become involved thereby rendering success, but also yielding greater success than He accomplished in His earthly ministry. How is this possible? It is achieved by the "Greater Works Principle."

~ GREATER WORKS PRINCIPLE ~

The "Greater Works" principle is an ingredient in fundamental evangelism truth that 21st century evangelists must believe. Simply stated, it says that 21st century evangelists must believe that they can accomplish more than Jesus did in His earthly ministry.

Listen, this must be a belief, or it will not work. That is not to say we will raise more lifeless bodies from the dead or cast out more demons...not at all. However, the "Greater Works" principle means we have opportunities to encounter more people than Jesus did. Therefore, with increased opportunities to interact with more people, we could very well supersede Jesus's earthly ministry numbers.

Watch this! During Jesus' earthly ministry, His mode of transportation was to either walk, ride a donkey, or travel by boat. Please note, there weren't any planes nor automobiles when Jesus was physically on earth. Therefore, the amount of geographical territory that Jesus covered in nearly four years of His ministry, we can now cover in less than four days and in some instances less than four hours!

Not convinced that we have more opportunities than Jesus did, well let's look at another area. When Jesus spoke, He did not have amplified sound or microphones to project His voice to a wider audience and a wider distance. I often wondered how the multitudes which followed Jesus heard His sermons without amplified sound? Especially those who were in the back.

I have preached without amplified sound, and it was a difficult task to project my voice where everyone in attendance could hear me. Surely, Jesus being the Son of God, maybe there was something supernatural which occurred to assist Him when He preached without audio. But if not, that would have been problematic for over five-thousand people to hear Him without a microphone, bullhorn, or any amplified sound. Perhaps some in attendance did not get the benefit of hearing the full message and left less impacted than others because they could not hear Jesus as he taught in that exact moment.

Therefore, we have greater opportunities to impact more lives based on our increased ability to be heard by everyone who attends our meetings. Because of microphone usage, the "Greater Works" principle is in effect because we have an advantage over Jesus when we use microphones. Our messages can be clearly heard by everyone in attendance.

As 21st century evangelists, we are not afraid to utilize technology to share the Gospel message. By employing technology, 21st century evangelists will reach far more people in less time than Jesus did and maybe even our evangelistic predecessors. We have remarkable opportunities to share the Gospel through technology and if desired, we can do this without even leaving the confines of our home.

Notice this, Jesus's ministry was centered in the Middle East.   i.e. Jerusalem, Capernaum, Galilee, Bethsaida, Samaria, Bethany, and Nazareth; it is estimated that Jesus' ministry span was about a 100-mile radius.   It would have taken Jesus's days if not weeks to travel to each region to share His messages. However, 21st century evangelists, via technologies like live stream video and podcasts, can be heard around the globe by the launch of a computer or through a cell phone.

Podcasts and live stream video applications have given 21st century evangelists opportunities to preach and teach in real time to people all over the world. Live stream applications allow 21st evangelists to be seen and heard by anyone who has an internet connection regardless of their geographical location.

I have used live streams and people from other countries viewed my videos within minutes of uploading them. That is remarkable because I may never visit their country, but my messages were sent and received, and it was not based on my ability to be physically present in that geographical area. That is amazing!

Technology is not the only advantage 21st century evangelists have to do greater works. There is also print media. We can use our pen or keyboard to do greater works and advance the Kingdom of God. When we write books, manuals, articles, post on social media, write movie scripts, editorials and etc. we have enacted the "Greater Works" principle.

Therefore, 21st century evangelists should not be intimidated by John 14:12 as long as John 14:13 confirms that Jesus will be with us, and He will do the work. Subsequently, we should be embolden as we endeavor to do "Greater Works' than Jesus and we must absolutely employ every tool and technological resource to spread the glorious Gospel message. We must be relentless!

PART TWO

EVANGELISM: THE EVENT

Chapter Five
~ Methods of Evangelism ~

Evangelism is defined as, "The art and method of sharing the Gospel." (LDJernigan, 2004)

Unlike the word "Evangelist," which is a noun because an evangelist is a person, the word "Evangelism" is a verb. Evangelism is about movement and action with the specific goal to share the Gospel of Jesus Christ.

Although there are various evangelism methods to get the Gospel of Jesus Christ into the ears and hearts of as many people as possible, the truth is that to be defined as evangelism, the Gospel must be included. Any event where the Gospel isn't presented is a mere community event. To be an authentic evangelism event, the Gospel must be presented in some form; that is the true definition and action form of evangelism, sharing and spreading.

There are several methods in which evangelism can be done. However, we will discuss three different methods of evangelism which I have found to be effective tools of evangelism: Individual, Relational, and Outreach.

~ INDIVIDUAL EVANGELISM ~

Individual evangelism is the most common method of evangelism. I refer to this as a "Cold-Call" encounter much like a telemarketer calling your phone without an invitation nor receiving consent prior to their call. This method can be invasive and is usually used by bold, courageous evangelistic people who are not afraid of rejection. Not every person in evangelism will be able to utilize this method.

Individual evangelism is where one person shares the Gospel with others, but unannounced and uninvited into people's personal space. More often than not, the people involved are not acquainted with each other and this can be their first introduction to one another.

Individual evangelism most utilized method is "door-to-door" evangelism. This is where an area or block was selected and people ring doorbells and randomly enter businesses to interact with people on the street to share the Gospel with whomever responds warmly or answers the door. The "door-to-door" method was commonly used by Jehovah Witnesses which is probably why most people are not receptive to this method.

The second most common method of individual evangelism is when a person distributes Christian literature with the hope of sharing the Gospel. Formerly known as "passing out tracks," but today we call the dispersed literature "Bait cards."

Bait cards are informative cards, bigger than a business card but smaller than a postcard, with a graphic Christian message which highlights Jesus and His salvation provision for humanity. In addition, bait cards can include church information i.e. Church name, address, phone number, website, logo, email address, QR code, social media handles, image of pastor/first family, and ministries/services the church offers.

Lastly, bait cards should include a call-to-action i.e. contact us, pray this prayer, return this card, or visit us. The call-to-action is an important section to include if you want to know if the evangelism efforts are effective. One way to measure evangelism effectiveness is by how people respond and by the feedback received. A call-to-action on a bait card can give statistical data needed for measurement of effectiveness.

Distributing tracks is not as popular today as it was years ago because being outside is not as safe as it once was. Consequently, when individual evangelism methods are employed, it's usually executed in well-lit and high traffic areas like retail, department, and grocery stores, or mall parking lots. Bus and train stations, sport events, and housing complexes are also good places for individual evangelism to distribute Christian literature.

Subsequently, I strongly recommend you choose highly populated areas for individual evangelism. Not just for safety reasons but also because those areas increase the probability of encountering large numbers of diverse people within a short period of time. This can be a productive way to share the Gospel and to hear the needs of the community.

One of the oldest, most common methods of individual evangelism is street preaching. Street preaching is highly effective because people hear the Gospel without church preliminaries and fluff. It's straight preaching which goes directly into the ears and instantly penetrates into the heart of listeners

Street preaching requires boldness from the preacher because satan moves through some listeners to antagonize, intimidate, and they try to cause embarrassment. Satan does this because he hates God and does not want the Gospel heard because people's faith in Jesus is increased when they hear the Gospel. That makes the devil mad, so he tries to stop street preaching by any means necessary.

*"So then _faith_ cometh by _hearing_*

and hearing by the word of God."
Romans 10:17 (KJV)

Street preaching is a spiritual assignment one must be graced to execute. Not every evangelist is called to street preaching. However, those who are called, have an anointing to instantly affect the heart, spirit, and even the mood of hearers.

When doing street preaching, you'll need amplified sound like a portable microphone, loudspeaker, or a bullhorn to be heard as there is noise on the streets i.e. cars, emergency vehicle sirens, music playing, and etc. Amplified sound increases the probability of people hearing the message and responding to the message. It's very difficult to preach on the streets without amplified sound.

In addition, with street preaching you should have an iPad, Kindle, a clipboard, or another way to collect data i.e. names, email addresses, phone numbers, and prayer requests. You want to collect data because you can follow up on prayer requests and prayers prayed. This is critically important if people invited Jesus into their heart for the first time during street preaching. You want to follow up with them and do your best to connect with them so they can grow in their Christian faith as a new believer. In addition, you can also use the collected data to create a database to send invitations of future meetings/events and to disperse additional ministry information. This can be another means of connection to build community.

Often street preaching is non-churched people's first encounter with the Gospel message; it can instigate tons of questions as first timers try to understand it. In addition, the Gospel is hard to digest within the couple minutes one has during street preaching, before the people move on with their activities. This makes every word, every sentence, and every paragraph in street preaching important! It is potent and packed with immense power to arrest people's attention and alter destinies within minutes. This is why street preaching is important and necessary and should never cease.

~ RELATIONAL EVANGELISM ~

Relational evangelism is another common method of evangelism. It mirrors individual evangelism as it also employs a one-on-one technique. However, the one-on-one technique is conducted with someone that is known to the person and has a prior connection and relationship.

Relational evangelism can be a wife evangelizing a husband or vice-versa. A parent sharing the Gospel with a child(ren) or grandchild(ren). Aunt, uncles, cousins, nieces or nephews sharing the Gospel with each other. Even best friends and co-workers can benefit from relational evangelism!

Most Christians do not enjoy relational evangelism and tend to find it discouraging primarily because the people with whom you share the Gospel with are familiar with the *old* you before you became a Christian. After becoming a Christian, one attempts to evangelize people they know through relational evangelism, but the people intended to be evangelized rejects the efforts. In fact, some will bring up your past to discourage you from sharing the Gospel with them.

In addition, relational evangelism can be time-consuming and take a while, sometimes years before you see the fruit of your labor, especially with a spouse and children. However, we must not be fainthearted about relational evangelism because it is the most successful method of evangelism! Yes, when we evangelize family/close friends, even though it takes time for them to decide, once they accept Jesus into their heart, they tend to remain with Him because they made a sober, well-thought-out decision, separate from emotions.

Therefore, relational evangelism is the most effective method of evangelism because (1) it is not an impulsive emotional decision and (2) they are persuaded by what they came to know about Jesus prior to accepting Him as their Savior and Lord. This is why we must not relent nor retreat when it comes to evangelizing families/friends. It works and is the most successful evangelistic method.

Look at Acts 1:8 (KJV)
*"But ye shall receive **power**, after that the Holy Ghost is come upon you: and ye shall be witnesses unto me **both** in **Jerusalem**, and in **all Judaea**, and **in Samaria**, and unto the uttermost part of the earth."*

The passage in Acts 1:8 is Jesus speaking before He returned back to God after His crucifixion, death, burial, and resurrection. These were the last earthly words of Jesus…we will receive power to witness! My Goodness! Do you know what that means? That means witnessing/evangelizing was quite important to Jesus to have this as His last earthly spoken words.

However, Jesus gave a blueprint for *how* we are to evangelize…we are to start in Jerusalem, which is symbolically home. We are to take the Gospel home first!

"And that repentance and remission of sins should be preached in his name among all nations, beginning at Jerusalem."

Luke 24:47 (KJV)

After we become Christians and receive the Holy Spirit, our job is to witness to our family and close friends first. Yes, we become employed by Jesus to evangelize...and not exclusively Christians inside of the church, but rather every Christian is mandated to witness or share their Christian faith, beginning with their family and friends outside and unconnected to the church.

Because we neglected to evangelize our family and close friends, that oversight has left the state of our families in disarray. If you are like me, you have family members who can benefit from the life-changing power of God. They cannot and should not be neglected so that we can preach to others who are not part of our Jerusalem. We must take the Gospel home!

Our family members experience negative consequences from addictions, sickness, poverty, depression, and sexual perversion. It is probable that if we employ relational evangelism one-person at a time, our families will experience transformation through the regenerative power of the Holy Spirit, and we can alter destinies and reverse curses.

For years I traveled as an itinerant evangelist and evangelized thousands of people and liberated the family of others, while my own family was caught in the clutches of satan. God revealed to me that I went to the end of the Scripture first by evangelizing the "uttermost part of the earth" before I went home to Jerusalem. I made intentional moves to reverse this and expose my family to God's true power.

Again, relational evangelism is about evangelizing those who means the most to us...*first*! Jesus wants our families and friends saved, healed, and delivered before we go to the nations and save the world. We must use our power to witness to our Jerusalem, *first*.

Planning an Outreach

It would be tragic to end this book without giving practical points on how to "Plan an Outreach."

Community outreaches are a major part of Christian evangelism but often the results are minimal. Churches have spent thousands upon thousands of dollars on outreaches which yielded little fruit and fell short of the desired results, no new converts nor additional church connections.

However, there are practical methods to use when planning outreaches which will enhance the overall success of the event. Most unsuccessful outreaches lacked clear vision and means to execute the vision; money and people. Unfortunately, after a few failed outreach attempts, discouragement will appear and soon the passion for outreach will disappear. It will seem like wasted time and money.

When the objective is to host an outreach to serve the "Least in society" as defined in Matthew 25:35-36 (sick, hungry, thirsty, homeless, naked/clothes, and prison), Jesus will be involved, and success will be attainable because of Him.

The overall motivation of evangelistic outreaches must be to compassionately serve those 6-outreach areas which Jesus defined in Matthew 25:35-36 (sick, hungry, thirsty, homeless, naked/clothes, and prison); it is those who need the most help with both natural and spiritual resources. Jesus called them the "Least of these" or the least in society. Why are they the "Least?" Probably because they have nothing to offer society and when society has nothing to gain, they tend to overlook and discard. However, Jesus instructed Christians to be different and remember the "Least" in society and serve them because His heart is with them too.

This will move the Kingdom of God forward and should increase visibility of a local church/ministry. This must be an intentional, focal point communicated from top-tier leaders to the entire team and throughout the entire ministry. When that is done, mixed with strategic planning and properly allocated resources (people and money), the possibility for the outreach to be successful will increase by 1000%.

1. Identify the "End-Goal" of the Outreach

The end-goal will guide the event from beginning-end. Without a pre-determined goal, you will find yourself spending less time on major things and more time on minor things. When this happens, days/hours before the event, you will discover the necessary tasks have not been completed. That will cause anxiety and stress.

In addition, with a clear end-goal, boundaries are established early, and decisions are made in the direction of the end-goal. This eliminates squandered time and financial waste, and it will preserve all resources primarily momentum.

2. Create a Budget

After you determine *why* the outreach is needed, a budget must be created. The budget will focus you and allow you to discover the *needs* of the outreach vs. the *wants* of the outreach. Without an itemized, detailed budget, the propensity to overspend or to spend on unnecessary items are greatly increased. The budget will unify the entire team because everyone will march to the same drumbeat.

3. Construct a Team

A team is needed when planning outreaches! Those people who refuse to work within a team environment are often immature and/or desire to take all the credit for themselves. They may call it independence, but it's actually linked to pride and an elevated thought that they're the only one who can get the job done well. Surely, they may get momentary satisfaction the day of the outreach by people praising them, but the cost was exhaustion and burnout; that is a great price to pay. Therefore, get a team and pull on the strengths of others to reach the end-goal of the outreach.

4. Set a Date

Dates are critical to an outreach. Holidays are not good days to host an outreach as most people spend time with family or travel on or around holidays. I recommend the week prior to the holiday or the week after the holiday as the best time to host an outreach.

Avoid holding your community outreach on special city-wide days. Most people will opt to attend the city-wide affair over your event because usually the city outreach may have better entertainment, food, and gifts.

Set a date which works best for your team, the church/ministry, and/or key prominent people you will invite. Be flexible with dates to gain the most from the outreach i.e. attendance, entertainments, giveaways, and food. You do not want to spend money and time on decorations, food, gifts, and etc. and few people show up because you chose the wrong date for your event.

5. Choose a Location
The location where the outreach will be held is also a critical component to consider. When possible, avoid using the church (inside) premises to hold outreaches but rather choose a neutral location. When non-believers come to church to get resources, they come with their defenses up because they expect to be bombard with sermons. The greetings, smiles, interactions, and messages all seem superficial and fake. The people come prepared to resist it, all of it. But when the outreach is held in a park, school auditorium, city hall, gymnasium or a community center, the participants are more relaxed, their defenses are down, expressions of love are received, and the Gospel becomes easier to share.

6. Plan the Details
Do not simply plan the food and gifts but give attention to smaller issues such as: who will set up the tables and organize the chairs, cook the food, pick up the trash, host the games, monitor the children, clean up, and etc. Usually it is not the 'big' issues that derail an outreach. It is usually the 'little' but important issues that causes an outreach to snag. Therefore, you want to plan the details. This is where a team can be beneficial because they will see things you may overlook.

In addition, planning the details are important because some non-believers make judgments about God and the local host church/ministry based on the level of excellence they experience at the outreach. Therefore, do not miss the opportunity to represent God well and the opportunity to add numerically to your local church by being sloppy. Plan the details, even the small and insignificant details!

7. Properly Position Volunteers

Position volunteers according to their strengths. Do not place someone where you desire them to be but rather ask your volunteers where they desire to serve. When volunteers are placed where they choose to serve, they are more pleasant to work with and produce more. Since most outreaches are held outside and can be lengthy, it is advised that volunteers are given the positions of their choice to avoid becoming disgruntled by the end of the outreach.

The most cordial, friendly, and reliable team members should be placed in high-demand areas. Team members should rotate every 45-60 minutes to relieve volunteers and give everyone an opportunity to experience all areas of the outreach; and take bathroom breaks too. Team members should also serve volunteers (water, food, napkins and etc) and display compassionate love for all volunteers. Verbally communicate to volunteers how they are appreciated and valued for their volunteer service, especially if they served in inclement weather or took time from work/family to volunteer.

It is important to verbally appreciate all volunteers and to give incentives such as T-shirts, reserved parking, wristbands, tumblers etc. You want volunteers to feel that they are VIP and greatly appreciated, even though they are unpaid volunteers

8. Collect Data

Create a means to collect data from participants. This is a Biblical practice because in Matthew 14 and 15, Jesus fed five-thousand and four thousand people. How do we know the number of people Jesus fed? Could it be that the disciples (or someone in Jesus' camp) collected data?

When we collect data, it keeps us accountable to God (we must follow up) and it tells us if our outreach is effective. For example, if we spend money to feed three hundred people and only seventy-five people were fed, then that data can be useful in planning the next outreach.

In addition, to collect data helps build relationship with those who attended the outreach. It is always a good idea to collect names, mailing address, email address, and a phone number from participants upon entering the outreach (or have an online or site registration). In addition, when possible, have participants to complete a 3-point questionnaire to help you learn the needs of the community and how to better serve them.

Incentives! People love free gifts, large or small. Therefore, it is a good idea to attach incentives to data collection and survey completions. Always inform participants that they will receive early notification of future events/outreaches (with discounts) because of the information they provided. Enter their names/ticket number in a raffle for a prize and/or give them a small keepsake at the end of the completion of registration or survey.

Before I conclude this section, there are a few things we must never do at an evangelism outreach. I have seen these things happening while out serving with believers. Although their intentions were good but overall, the list below are not best practices during an outreach.

1. Do not give money. Recipients at an outreach will have needs, visible needs but you are there to distribute what was marketed on the flyer and what's available. Do not go on a personal crusade and give people money from your own pocket. Stay within the confines of the outreach and distribute what was approved by the leaders and the team.

2. Do not distribute your own literature or promote your ministry or organization. That is unethical! Only disperse approved literature and information made available by the outreach host. Their outreach is not a networking opportunity for you nor your ministry/organization.

3. Do not wonder off alone to interact privately with an attendee at the outreach. This is dangerous! Always remain with 2-3 people. Even when going to the bathroom, others should be informed of your whereabouts. It is not control or dominance, it is about safety and accountability.

4. Do not bring your own resources (food, gifts) unless approved by the host of the outreach. This can cause separation and disunity among the team.

Although it may be good intentions, it may not fit into the overall goal of the outreach.

5. Do not invite others to speak or promise them microphone time. This can only be approved by the organizers and should not be an impromptu add-on because you want to score points with someone i.e. a politician, pastor, or etc.

LEAD SOMEONE TO JESUS

It is *critically* important that we encourage non-believers to invite Jesus into their hearts to become believers of Jesus Christ. This should not only occur during a Sunday morning service but also during outreaches, street evangelism ministry, and whenever given the opportunity.

Most Christians are intimidated to suggest people make a decision for Jesus primarily because they themselves are not confident in leading them to the Lord. For this reason, I included this portion in this manual because I too have experienced fear when it was time for me to lead someone to Jesus. The more I studied, it became clear that in Romans 10:9-10, God left us a blueprint to follow when we lead someone to Jesus; and, it's quite simple...

> *"That if thou shalt **confess** with thy mouth the Lord Jesus,*
> *and shalt **believe** in thine heart that God*
> *hath raised him from the dead, thou shalt be **saved**.*
> *For with the heart man **believeth** unto righteousness;*
> *and with the mouth **confession** is made unto salvation."*
> Romans 10:9-10 (KJV)

According to Romans 10:9-10, there are only a few simple steps needed when leading someone to Jesus.

1. Confess with Mouth the "Lord Jesus."

Every person who made a decision to receive God's free gift of salvation by placing their faith in Jesus Christ must confess it. They must verbally confess with their mouth!

Many denominations have blundered this step. Oftentimes the pastor recites a prayer and ask the individual to answer "Yes or No." The individual usually nods their head or say, "Yes." Although that has been a practice for decades, that practice is

NOT Biblical...the individual must verbally confess with their own mouth, and not just nod their head in agreement.

They must confess "The Lord Jesus!" This is extremely important because there is no other name by which people can be saved (Romans 4:12), therefore they must confess the Lord Jesus. He is the Way, the Truth, and the Life. Jesus is the *only* way to God the Father, therefore everyone must confess "The Lord Jesus."

In addition, some people like to hide behind the neutral term of "God." Every religious entity has a variation of God or a deity they worship. Therefore, as Christians we are specific about who we pledge our allegiance to by using His name...Jesus! We must ensure that people who make a decision for Jesus are aware they are deciding to become a follower of Jesus Christ and no other God. They must confess "The Lord Jesus!"

2. Believe in Heart, God raised Jesus from the Dead
Our entire Christian faith rests on the fact that Jesus was raised from the dead. Without His resurrection, Jesus would simply be another powerful man who died. With the resurrection, Jesus separates Himself from every other religious leader who died because He is the only one who was resurrected and now He lives...Glory to God!

Therefore, every person who makes a decision to be saved, must verbally express belief in Jesus' resurrection through God's power.

3. Thou shalt be saved
A verbal confession and belief in the heart are the only Biblical prerequisites to salvation. Some denominations have addendums which cannot be supported Biblically but rather it's just someone's interpretation of salvation. However, the Bible gives

us the requirements for salvation…Confess and believe, nothing more or and nothing less.

SAMPLE PRAYER

This is a sample prayer to have an individual who desires to invite Jesus into their heart to repeat. Do NOT utilize this prayer verbatim on every occasion. As the situation may change from person-to-person, you will need to be led by the Holy Spirit on how to lead each individual person. This prayer is only a template...

"Lord Jesus, I am a sinner, and I recognize I need a savior. I ask for forgiveness of all my sins and to be cleansed of every bad action I have ever committed. Jesus, I confess with my mouth, and I believe in my heart that you came, died, and on the third day, God raised you from the dead; therefore, according to Romans 10:9-10 I am saved. I thank you Jesus, that I am now saved and will live with you in eternity, forever."

Remember, ask the individual to repeat *after* you and keep the prayer short! The entire prayer should be completed in less than one minute. You do not want to overwhelm the person by being long-winded and overdoing it.

Recite one line at a time and speak slowly and loud enough for them to hear you. Pause for a few seconds to give them time to repeat your words. If they do not hear or repeat your words, do not move forward, but rather repeat that line until they say it. When the entire prayer has been completed, assure them that they are saved and rejoice with them!

However, your job is not yet complete. Always encourage them to connect with a community of believers where they can grow spiritually. Explain to them that a Christian community will assist in their spiritual growth much like food assists in their natural growth. If possible, get basic information from them and follow-up with them within 1-2 days to answer any questions they may have.

About Linda D. Jernigan, M.A.

Pastor Linda D. Jernigan, M.A., was born on the Westside of Chicago, IL. She is the youngest of eight children. Pastor Linda was endorsed as an evangelist in October 2006.

As a former high school dropout, Pastor Linda received her Master's Degree in Communications in 2012 and she adamantly declares her faith in God and her academic accomplishments as the catalyst for the socio-economic success she currently experiences. Pastor Linda has penned seven literary works, written two manuals, produced two deliverance DVD's, appeared on innumerous television and radio shows, been featured, and quoted in several newspapers/magazine articles. Pastor Linda has led a myriad of community outreaches throughout Chicago and nationally where countless people have been empowered and encouraged as she demonstrated the love of Jesus through her evangelistic outreaches.

Pastor Linda has traveled extensively from her home city of Chicago throughout America and Europe preaching the Gospel of salvation and deliverance to everyone who is gripped in the clutches of satan; evangelizing and admonishing them to pursue authentic, long-term, sustained deliverance through unshakable faith and trust in Jesus Christ.

Made in the USA
Monee, IL
08 April 2025

15433722R00080